Table of Contents

PART 1: HYGGE HOME
INTRODUCTION 1
CHAPTER 1 3
THE BASICS OF HYGGE AND THE HOME 3
CHAPTER 2 6
CREATING A FUNCTIONAL SPACE AND DECIDING ITS FUNTION 6
CHAPTER 3 10
CHAPTER 4 14
UNDERSTANDING THE MEANING OF ITEMS 14
CHAPTER 5 18
EASE OF ACCESS MEANS PEACE OF MIND 18
CHAPTER 6 21
DEALING WITH LIGHT IN THE HOME AND HYGGE 21
CHAPTER 7 27
SPACE IN AND AROUND THE HOME 27
CHAPTER 8 29
CLUTTER AND THE STRESS OF LIFE AND DE-CLUTTERING FOR MINDFULNESS 29
CHAPTER 9 32
ORGANIZING EACH ROOM 32
CHAPTER 10 36
BRINGING THE OUTSIDE IN 36
CHAPTER 11 40
BRINGING PEACE TO THE HOME VIA DECORATING 40
CHAPTER 12 44
USEFUL TIPS FOR EACH ROOM IN THE HOME 44
CHAPTER 13 48
SUMMING THINGS UP 48

PART 2: HYGGE LIVING 53
INTRODUCTION: PEACEFUL, COZY LIVING 54
CHAPTER 1 56
THE ORIGINS OF HYGGE AND ITS MEANING 56
CHAPTER 2 60
UNDERSTANDING THE ART OF MINDFULNESS 60
CHAPTER 3 65
BRINGING HYGGE INTO THE HOME 65
CHAPTER 4 73

Bringing Hygge into the Home 73
Chapter 5 77
Friends and Their Role in Your Life 77
Chapter 6 83
The Idea of Experiences 83
Chapter 7 88
Hygge can Extend to the Workplace 88
Chapter 8 93
Adding Some Comfort into Your Life 93
Chapter 9 100
Bringing it All Together 100
Conclusion 103

My Free Gift to You 106

About The Author 107

Part 1: Hygge Home

Keep Your Home Life Simple with Danish Living Concepts

Introduction

Picture this for a moment. Walking in your front door after a hard day at work filled with stress and pressure, you are greeted by a comfortable, relaxing space where you can unwind at your leisure.

Sound idyllic?

Well, the problem is that so many people are unable to do that. They are unable to come home and feel as if they are surrounded by peace and serenity, because they have not created that kind of atmosphere.

That is an absolute crying shame. We should all be able to go home and feel as if it is our own perfect little space. We should have areas where the pressures and stresses of the outside world simply drift away as we cocoon ourselves with peace, serenity, and a calming atmosphere.

But how? Where do you even begin?

Well, that's where this book is going to prove to be useful. This book is all about helping you to create that very atmosphere. It's all about helping you to bring some order to your home, creating space so you can breathe, and incorporating those little hints of comfort and peacefulness that can end up meaning the world to you.

This book is all about hygge, the Danish concept of cozy and comfortable living. It's not about materialism or boasting about what you have in life. It's more about the essence of an object and what it can bring to you and your life.

Throughout this book, we will guide you on how to de-clutter and de-stress your home and, as a result, your life as well. We will guide you as to how to remove those objects that no longer mean that much or are taking up space and how to create that comforting setting that you have been dreaming about.

The Danes are voted the happiest nation in the world and when you consider that they come from a country that has harsh winters and hours of darkness, then that's an impressive feat. It's a feat that is known to have been achieved thanks to the concept of hygge. If it's capable of making them happy with their lives and their homes, then surely it's worth exploring.

So, what are we going to do?

Well, there are many different aspects of hygge and how to apply its concepts in your home, so we have a lot to get through. However, there's no pressure being applied as that in itself could be classed as being anti-hygge, and what would be the point in that?

We are going to take you on a journey through your home and help you to apply the rules and concepts of hygge wherever possible. There are going to be some changes that need to be made, but at the end of the day your home will be far more peaceful and serene than ever before.

With hygge, you get out what you put into it, but the one thing we do recommend right from the outset is that you invest your heart and soul from the start. After all, hygge is intended to help those two very things.

Take a deep breath and prepare yourself for something that is going to bring you a sense of calm that you thought you would never be able to achieve.

Chapter 1

The Basics of Hygge and the Home

Before one begins this delightful journey into 'Hygge' and the home, there has to be some sort of understanding about *hygge* and what it means. Also, one might ask why the world suddenly made an *old traditional* style of living a *buzz word*, something new and exciting, something special and different?

The word hygge is pronounced as 'Hoo oogah,' and while pronunciation is pretty easy to impart to a reader, the actual meaning is a little more complex.

In today's world where everything appears to be busier, faster, and more intricate, hygge's very simplicity has become hard to assimilate or to understand. However, by focusing on the home throughout this book, you will begin to bring together the various aspects of this Danish approach to the way of living and start to employ them in your own home.

There is no direct translation for hygge, and this is perhaps why it is both special and elusive. Hygge is mostly about comfort, a mindful approach to anything and everything, a certain coziness, an earnest simplicity that warms the hearts of friends and family alike. Surely this is something that you would love to apply to your own home and personal surroundings?

Warmth being key, since hygge is a part of life in most Scandinavian countries and as many people know there is little warmth or light for the majority of the year. Cold, bleak landscapes are touched by the warmth and pleasure of what is primarily a state of mind followed by a set of actions. It's no surprise that the home, and making a home as cozy as possible, is at the absolute root of hygge.

Hygge is not singularly attributed to cold weather; it can be enjoyed in any season. In fact, enjoying the seasons is really part of hygge, too.

In this book, hygge is taken apart gently and placed neatly into our life and into your home.

The home is where we are nurtured, sustained, loved and cared for, no matter our personal situation. We could have a large family, an interestingly diverse family, or we could be living on our own, such is the world today. However, the principles remain the same, and the outcome also remains the same.

Hygge is not prescriptive. It is not judgmental. It is everything you've learned undone and redone. It is a little like going back to basics and to the things that matter to us. It is a beauty that does not cost money, does not entertain debt, and does not pressure people into living a certain way. It is a way of life that nurtures and gently wraps each individual in a life blanket making them feel loved, cared for, and appreciated.

In a world survey, it was discovered that Danish people are one of the most happiest groups of people in the world. This might be hard to get one's mind around, since as mentioned earlier Denmark is clothed for the most part of the year in a semi-dark coat of what could be considered bleakness. It's no surprise that the home then forms an integral part of hygge and that the Danes do their best to make it as comforting as possible.

Let us consider this when reading the above sentence. Add some lanterns, laughter, and friends to this bleak landscape and what do you have? You have a certain kind of magic that can easily be applied to your own personal space. Each element is important because without bleakness, the lanterns could not spill their warm, comforting light upon the gray snow, illuminating it into silver shimmering plateaus. This is the stuff that dreams are made of. This is where happiness resides. Also, can you just imagine the positive feelings you would have coming home from work and knowing that you will encounter that kind of happiness the moment you walk through your front door?

There is a certain kind of 'letting go' involved in hygge. Letting go of ideas, objects, thoughts and ideation's that do not serve us. It is also a little bit about delving into our very core and understanding what our priorities are, and then creating a life that is worthwhile and happy for us. However, the only way in which you can really hope to achieve this is by starting with your own home. Hygge allows you to create that calm atmosphere where you wake up and feel ready to start the day as you aren't surrounded by that chaos that is common in the world.

In the chapters that follow, the home is the focus of hygge and also the heart. The home as mentioned before is the place where we can begin our journey—a journey of peaceful harmony that will spill out to all other areas of our lives.

We will understand that clutter, useless objects, and materialism are overrated. Find happiness in the smaller, simpler things in life. Happiness and contentment cannot be bought, but they can be learned to an extent.

The home is where we can create ourselves, create our own ideal space, and learn more about ourselves and how to become peaceful in mindfulness. How on earth can you ever hope to do that if you are not in what you determine to be your ideal space? By adopting these Danish methods in each and every room, you can start to create that sense of solace that you have been craving.

By de-cluttering, understanding what a room should really be used for, by allowing easy access to everything you need, and a real sense of organization, you will bring that calmness to your home. Now, how good does that sound? Are you ready to incorporate those ideas into your own life?

Each person's idea of a comfortable, peaceful home is different, and all of this will be taken into account. It is really about putting what you already know deep inside of you into concrete form. It is also a bit about searching within in order to find a new way of living away from the hustle and bustle of life, but more importantly it's about living life your way—the way that makes you happy.

Chapter 2

Creating a Functional Space and Deciding its Funtion

Now that you have a better understanding of the basic concepts of hygge and its connection to your home, we can start to take things further to help you in the implementation of the various aspects. By doing so, you will eventually find yourself living in a space that is not only your own but is functional, calming, and serves its purpose, no matter what that may be.

You have to admit, that does sound pretty special.

Getting Things Started
The first thing for you to do is to consider the space as this plays a central role in hygge. You may think that your home is already all laid out with different ideas for the rooms, but are you actually happy with them? Does it lend to the overall flow of your home? More on that later.

You also need to think about each room on a smaller scale and as an individual. Not sure what we mean? Well, let's explain it a bit better.

Take the living room as an example; you may even be sitting in your own living room as you read this e-book. Look around you and what do you see? How do you see the function of the room? Does it serve every purpose that you think you will need in this room? How does it feel to you? Is it comforting or does it have no real character? Is it lacking soul?

Don't worry; it's not as bad as it sounds at this point.

For most people, a living room will provide a space to entertain guests. There may be a stereo and speakers, a television is pretty much guaranteed, and all of this means that the space has a function. There will also be comfortable chairs for people to relax on and you may have even thought about how the chairs are positioned so that everybody can see one another without any difficulties.

However, are you missing out on anything?

Look at each corner or the space by the fireplace. Are they being used or are they just left abandoned and vacant? If this is the case, then you aren't doing it right, and something needs to be addressed.

This is not to say that each part of a room needs to have its use, but what use is the living room if you have things that are potentially noisy and yet you want some peace and quiet? You have your comfortable chairs in the living room. You can have the warm, snug fire on in the winter keeping you cozy so why would you then have to go elsewhere if you wanted that peaceful setting?

This is where the concept of space and functionality comes into its own. That is where the concept of hygge can effectively come to your rescue.

Taking the Concept of Functional Space Further
At this point, we will stay in the living room, although the ideas and concepts that we are discussing can easily be applied to different rooms throughout your home.

Stand in the doorway to your living room and look around you. Where are things situated? Can you access everything in the room without too much difficulty? Are there points that you just do not use?

Do you find that as you move around the room, you are constantly banging into things as the place is overcrowded? Does the room bring you any kind of peace or serenity?

There are a number of questions that need to be addressed here, but they are all pertinent if you are serious about adopting hygge into your life and your home. There should be a sense of flow, a feeling of ease as you move around. You should be aware of what the purpose is of any given space at any given time, or even just what it could be turned into in an instant.

Hygge teaches you that there is no point in having that dining table and chairs if it's crushed into a corner never to be used. It gets even worse if the table top is covered in objects and just taking up space. There's no point in having a room that feels as if it is almost going to suffocate you because of the multitude of objects that are contained within it.

But how do you change this? What approach is best for you to take?

Well, the entire idea of this chapter is just to get you thinking about not only each room but each corner of the room along with each object. You need to do this in accordance with the principles of mindfulness as that alone is known to soothe the mind.

Drawing Up Your Plan of Functionality
With hygge, there is a real sense of you putting some thought into each action and decision that you make in your home. Doing things in a rushed manner without thinking about it is just a sign of the chaotic world that we tend to live in—a world that we are so desperately trying to extract ourselves from.

It's fair to assume that if our home life is chaotic and without function, then the rest of our life is probably the same. There is a need for you to feel connected to the space. That you, and anybody else, is able to identify what the space is for and are free to use it for that purpose.

How can that happen if you have no idea what is actually going on?

Now, we aren't saying that you need to walk around the home like some kind of surveyor and spend an extraordinary length of time studying all of this, but by the same measures, this isn't something to be done in an instant.

You see, a plan of functionality ties in with something that we will be addressing later on, which is organization and space in accordance with the ideas of hygge. However, you need to know the function of a room to then know how to organize it, or else you will just confuse yourself from the outset.

Also, this is not something that you can do on your own. Instead, there has to be a consultation with everyone that will be using the space, or you can easily find one individual not best pleased with a room, and those negative feelings are not in accordance with what you are hoping to achieve.

The Conclusion Regarding Functionality
It's understandable if you feel that this entire concept of functionality is rather confusing as it can be a difficult idea to get a grip on at first. However, as it plays a central role in the entire idea of hygge in and around the home, then you need to spend time studying it.

To help, these points are the key things to always have at the forefront of your mind, and knowing them may make it easier for you to move forward and apply the rules to your own home.

- Functionality means you know what the room is being used for.
- Consider breaking down the room into smaller areas and their function.
- Remember, a room can have more than one function.
- Have a clear idea of where things will go in a room.
- Once you understand the functionality, you can then start to work on the space.
- Objects are related to the functionality.

As we said, when you are aware of the function of a space, you are then able to move onto the next point, which is starting to deal with your belongings and, once again, this is an important part of hygge.

Chapter 3

Coming to Terms with Objects and Moving Items On

From the previous chapter, you should have started to gain an idea of the important role that is being played by objects and their function in the entire approach to hygge. In this chapter, we will explore the role of objects even further.

Here, we stress the importance of allowing certain objects to move on and not to feel bad about it. After all, feeling bad about something is not exactly working along with the concept of mindfulness as you enter a dark cycle of sadness, and that is the antithesis of what hygge is all about.

So, let's explore objects in your home and life a bit further and see how you can prepare yourself for potentially letting go. Remember, often the letting go part is the hardest stage, but once you get through it, the sense of freedom that you experience makes it all feel worthwhile.

This is something that can take some time for you to work through, but work through it you must if you do indeed aspire to fully embrace hygge in and around your home. Of course, the length of time it will take is dependent on how large your home is and also how many objects you own, but the concepts stay the same regardless.

Looking at the Objects
The length of time it will take to go through objects in your home will vary depending on what you own, but the concept remains the same.

In Denmark, it is not generally accepted in society for people to own a number of different items. This extravagance is frowned upon by society, so it's unusual for homes to be as full as they tend to be in other countries. However, they are still going to look at the objects that are in their possession and fully assess their role in the home.

Their normal approach is that you only own what you need. For the Danes, this approach is more important than the price they pay for items.

That being said, what should your approach be with your own objects?

Well, the first thing is to actually take stock of what you have. You need to be aware of the objects you own, as this is the only way in which you can then ever hope to decipher their functionality or purpose and how it fits into your plans for each room.

To do this, you must try and move past the concept of just 'liking' an object because feeling this way is different to it having a purpose.

Think of these questions before you go any further:

- How much do I like it?
- What is its role?
- Does it fit in with the proposed function of the room?
- Is it the only one I have, or do I have more of the same?
- Do I have similar objects elsewhere in the home?

We are talking about some very basic questions, and yet they can make it so much easier for you to come to an understanding of what objects you should perhaps hold onto and those objects that may be best served elsewhere.

However, even when it comes to throwing out objects or moving them on, the Danes don't do it without any thought. We will look at this next.

Moving Items on in the Correct Manner
Finally, we have to quickly mention the importance of moving the items on in the correct manner. You see, most of us have a tendency to just throw things in the trash once we have finished with them, but is that the correct thing to do?

It's perhaps best to remember the saying 'another man's trash is another man's treasure' because that phrase in itself is hygge. Just because you no longer require it doesn't mean that everybody else will feel the same way.

So, how do you move items on in the correct manner if you aren't just throwing them away? Well, it's all to do with your state of mind at the time and the thoughts that go into the entire process.

You need to understand that there is a very strong concept of sharing in hygge and this is something that all Danes will do, and there's no doubt that it does bring its own sense of happiness. However, most of us will have never thought about doing it with items we own, and this is a shame.

For the Danes, there is a sense of enjoyment in moving items on to a new home, whether it be donating to a charity or giving the object to a friend or relative that has expressed their love or desire for the object. Either of these options brings with it real satisfaction, and then you have the added benefit of knowing that the item is no longer cluttering up your space.

In other words, you are going to win on more than one level.

Completing the Initial Analysis of Objects in the Home
We will be spending more time looking at objects in different areas throughout this book. However, at this point, our main focus has been on just trying to get you prepared for looking at what you own.

Only a small percentage of people actually do this, and that's one reason why we have this amazing ability to accumulate 'stuff.'

Thanks to their approach, the Danes manage to avoid this particular issue as they are aware of what they are looking for, how it fits in, and the role it plays before they spend money. Also, they understand if they already have something that will fit the bill, which does make life so much easier.

You will also find that they are methodical in how they go about things. They study objects, think about them, discuss them with others if required, and come to a well-considered opinion as to what should happen to it. If the item is to be moved on elsewhere, then they do so with a happy heart and thank the object for the service and pleasure it has given them.

If you pass on an object with a happy heart and have come to terms with the idea that it will then belong to someone else, then there's little chance of you regretting your decision later. That's also why they spend time being aware of their belongings as it then makes the decision to let it go so much easier to make.

So, to complete the analysis of what you have in your home, we recommend doing this:

- Work through the items in each room and be prepared to have a clear out.
- As before, check if you have more than one and, if so, do you need it?
- Consider if an object can be used elsewhere in the home.
- Accept if something has had its time with you.

Allow it to go elsewhere so it can be enjoyed and bring pleasure.

Chapter 4

Understanding the Meaning of Items

By understanding the actual meaning of items, it allows us to better find their purpose in our lives. Remember, we can all develop various attachments to items that do not actually serve any need, and yet that is often deemed to be enough for us to hold onto them for a ridiculous period of time.

The result is an accumulation of clutter that we have artificially attached ourselves to and that's not exactly going to make life easy for us when it comes to us trying to sort both your home and life out.

Of course, this should never lead to you just throwing objects out because you feel that you have to, just as we covered in the previous chapter. Instead, hygge in this context is all about being at one with the object and truly understanding what it means.

You are never going to throw everything out because you feel that you now need to adopt a minimalist lifestyle. That's not the idea at all.

So, what do you do?

Let's go through some examples.

Getting Back to Basics with Items

Often, one can have an item that has sentimental value, but where do those sentiments come from, and what is their role in your life? Does the item bring you happiness, or does it weigh you down with the expectation that you should keep it?

As you can imagine, the first part is following the idea of hygge, and being weighed down is very anti-hygge and should be avoided.

Now, this may seem to be a tiring issue to get involved in, but the truth is that working through the basic reasons behind you having an item can actually be rather healing. It can help you to release some inner emotions and feelings and bring a sense of happiness and fulfilment that may have otherwise been missing, and who could ever see that as being a bad thing?

Okay, that all sounds slightly hippy-esque, and it's otherwise been missing, and who could ever see that as being.

Often, we can have items in our possession that have little personal meaning to us. However, we feel obliged to hold onto them for fear of upsetting others. This will tend to lead to our homes being filled with objects that we don't want, and that alone is going to give us some stress.

To deal with this situation, you need to be prepared to spend time thinking carefully about each item and the role that it plays. We mentioned this in brief in the previous chapter, but thanks to the position it holds in the Danish concept of hygge and bringing peace to the home, it's worth talking about it again.

Looking at Objects More Closely

Here's the problem with items we own at any point in our lives. If we kept everything that we have ever liked, then we would need a mansion just to store everything. Our homes would be crammed full of objects that, to be honest, have no real role other than some kind of sentimental value that may even have been lost to us.

Now, we aren't saying that Danes don't have those sentimental feelings; they do. However, they are more honest in what objects mean to them whereas we tend to be absorbed by those thoughts that go through our mind.

So, how do we recommend that you do this? How do you bring hygge into your home and adopt the methods used by the Danes?

Well, thankfully it's easier than most expect, which should come as a relief to you. For most, the best approach is to actually begin with taking just one room at a time. Of course, you already know what your planned function is for that room, so life is easier.

When looking at your objects in a room, please do consider the following points just to make life that bit easier:

- When did I last use it?

- Is it serving a purpose?

- What difference does it make to my life?

- Does it fit in with the idea I have surrounding the function of the room?

Ascertaining what should be kept, what should be moved or re-purposed, and what should be disposed of is important.

Considering the Sentimental Value

We mentioned earlier in the chapter that the sentimental value of an object is important, but just how big a role does it play in your life?

It's clear that some people have attachments to objects more than others; we are all different, but you need to really get to the root of these thoughts and feelings before you can go any further.

This also applies to those family heirlooms that we seem to gather. Now, they will often have some kind of meaning, but do you really understand the true meaning? You would be surprised at how these items or those that we have a false sense of attachment to can clutter up our homes. All this does is add more items to a room and detracts us from the true function of the space.

So, what do you do? Well, as we have been doing throughout this book, there are a number of important points to consider and questions to ask yourself that should make this part smoother.

- Does it have genuine sentimental value, or is it forced on you?

- Is there another way you can keep the memory of the item?

- Is it serving a purpose?

- Does it fit in with the function of the room?

- Can it be moved elsewhere?

- What difference does it make to your life?

This isn't about clearing out things for the sake of it; there's more to it than that. However, the thing about hygge and the Danes is that they don't believe in having objects in their home if there's no genuine need for them. This is clutter, even if it means something to somebody else. We will look into clutter in another chapter.

Chapter 5

Ease of Access Means Peace of Mind

At this stage, we are building up to the point of where we take you through the entire de-cluttering concept, but in this chapter, it's more about the importance of mindfulness in the home and how that has an impact on decisions that you will then make.

However, what do we actually mean by peace of mind, and how does it fit into the concept of 'ease of access?' Admittedly, it does sound as if the two just cannot go together, but that's not the case at all. Instead, the two work in tandem. It's just a matter of knowing how.

Try to think of things from this perspective. A room in your home can also be a passageway to move between spaces. Now, do you want to have to walk around numerous items and step over obstacles to get from A to B?

Absolutely not, and that in itself is hardly going to bring you the peace of mind that you are seeking while adopting the methods of hygge in your life.

Taking the Concept of Ease of Access Further

Think about the Scandinavian design elements in the home for just one second. They have a tendency for everything to be well laid out and planned to absolute perfection. Each item of furniture has its place, and often they will have more than one function to further increase their usability.

We talk elsewhere in the book about flow, and this goes hand in hand with the point we are discussing now. To help, let's take these ideas out of the home for just a moment and think of a department store. Picture yourself walking in the door to be then faced with a number of counters selling various brand names and products.

Often, there is a flow between them, but more importantly, you can get to all of their items without encountering any problems. How frustrated would you be if displays were blocking what you were trying to get to? How would you react?

The answer is that you would probably react in a negative manner, including getting angry and fed up. Something that should have been pleasurable is no longer pleasurable. It has been replaced by a stressful situation, and that can then have an effect that hangs around in your mind for a considerable period of time.

The very same thing applies to your home.

Improving the Layout

So, how do you go about actually solving this particular problem?

Well, you have to remember the things we have looked at so far, which means the ability to understand the objects in your home and also the function of the different spaces. Without these two things, you stand no chance of actually being able to work at improving the access in a room, not to mention your overall home.

It's important that these things all work in tandem. Let's look at a room in the home as an example of how this can all come together.

To give some sense of continuity, we will look at the living room once again. Now, as you know, the living room has a number of different functions, and that is where the importance of layout and access comes into play.

Let's say that in your living room you have a stereo system, a television, chairs, and a fireplace. The aim of hygge is that you can use anything and everything in a room without too much effort.

This means you should be able to see the television from each chair without having to move it or change your angle to sit comfortably. Nobody should be sitting in direct line of the fire, so they are far too hot while everyone else is comfortable. Everybody should be capable of switching any devices on without having to lean over other objects. People should be able to get to their seats and feel relaxed. Lights should be able to be switched on and off without too much difficulty.

As you can see, the idea of looking at the layout of a room is that the function is fulfilled without things having to constantly be adjusted. That in itself is stressful and frustrating, and you can start to see how that is against hygge. Also, it makes perfect sense that the more cramped a room is because of clutter, then the harder it is to do all of these tasks without running the risk of knocking things over, having to move things, and just generally being annoyed.

So, when thinking about the ease of access concept, think about these points.

Can you access each piece of furniture without any difficulty?

Which objects obstruct you?

Can you use everything without having to alter the position of something?

Do you need to remove any object to improve access?

How comfortable is the room with what is in it at this point?

Can the function of the room be achieved with the items in that room?

This is all about making life as easy as possible. It's all about lowering your stress and getting rid of those objects that just get in the way. You want to use everything in your home without any difficulty.

Chapter 6

Dealing with Light in the Home and Hygge

Light is very, very important in hygge. In fact, its role cannot be stressed enough since light can have such an impact on the overall mood of your entire home while also relaxing you and allowing you to unwind.

However, keep this in mind: hygge originated in Denmark which, in winter, has a number of months where there are only a few hours of actual daylight, and this means the Danes have had to turn to alternative options for the sake of light.

Light is capable of bringing a sense of magic to the home. It can illuminate. It can bring comfort. It can completely change the mood and atmosphere of a room or even just a corner. It can also be used to differentiate between spaces that are for different purposes.

In other words, light is more powerful and useful than you may have initially thought.

Once again, we will look at examples to stress what you should be hoping to achieve with light. You want to create that cozy and comfortable atmosphere as much as possible, don't you?

Light and Leading into the Home

The art of hygge and your home begins from the moment you walk toward your house. How inviting does it look? Is the front dark and, to be frank, scary and intimidating?

Well, if it is, then you are missing the point already.

Walking up to your home should result in your house being well lit making it more appealing to guests. It should have an outdoor light at the front door that is also not too strong, giving it a warm glow. It's the kind of light that makes people feel welcome, while also giving your home the appearance of being alive. That, in itself, is a huge part of this entire process.

Also, as you enter your home, what would be the better option? A dark hallway waiting for you to remove your shoes and coat before you venture forth? Or, you open the front door and are welcomed by a warm space alongside a gentle light that provides a glow and a certain degree of richness?

Clearly, the second one is the most appealing for the majority of people, and you have to think about the way in which it makes you feel about the rest of your home. It should, by all accounts, make it easier to appreciate being home and that you have moved into your own space. It's amazing the difference in feelings that you can have just by using a light at this point.

But let's move into other rooms of the home and look at the way in which light can have a profound impact on the atmosphere.

Bright Light is Not Always Good

Too often, we have this mistaken belief that everything in our homes should be well lit, resulting in us sitting in a room that resembles the light in a sports stadium. However, the Danes do not entirely agree with this approach, and they have their own opinion of how light works in a home.

The one thing that they do love is natural light flooding in. There will often be light colored furniture, or mainly white, in order to allow the light to bounce off the surfaces and further illuminate the room. Windows can be large and uncluttered to allow the maximum amount of light to shine in for as long as possible.

However, things will often change when it comes to the dark evenings or while entertaining. At that point, light is not seen as being a functional tool to help you to see, but rather a tool to help add a certain ambiance to the room. This is something that the Danes have perfected over the years, and it really is down to a fine art.

To copy their approach, you need to study your lighting in each room. How many lights you need and how strong the wattage of the light bulbs can vary according to the size of the room, but you are going to find out that you actually need less than you initially thought.

Adopting the Hygge Lighting Methods

To perfect the hygge lighting methods and to then create a wonderful atmosphere in your home, it's important that you begin by turning on the various lights as you would normally do. After this, step back for a moment and observe the room. What do you see?

With this, you need to be able to stand back and actually look at the direction of the light. How much of the space does each light illuminate? Is it harsh or soft? What is the purpose of the light in its current position?

You need to become aware that the Danes will tackle light from a completely different perspective. They don't see it as just being a way to illuminate a room. Instead, it's more about using it in a clever manner to enhance what is already there, and to create a cozy and comfortable atmosphere.

They are still going to have those high wattage bulbs, but they are not the main light source and are merely there if required. They much prefer either lower wattage bulbs, fairy lights, and they are the biggest purchasers or candles in the world, which also tells you something else about their most preferred light source.

Also, a light needs to have a purpose, which is a recurring theme throughout this book, rather than just being stuck in the middle of the room and attempting to light every single corner at the one time.

However, the way in which light is applied to your rooms can be rather specific, so it's best we check that out next.

Applying it to Your Rooms

The Danish idea is to create special areas in the room due to light and that's easier to do than you may have been expecting. Once again, if we can think of the living room as an example, remembering that the same ideas can indeed be applied throughout the home.

To correctly apply lighting in the living room, you have to stand back and view the room as a whole. Look at the shape of it and where all of the items in the room are positioned. Also, you must think about the purpose of the room as this ties in with the kind of feelings and atmosphere that you will want to create. As light is playing a central role in this, it makes sense to have a firm idea of this before you begin.

The main things that you will be using in this instance are; small lights with lower wattage bulbs, candles of various sizes, and also fairy lights. You might even lights that can stick onto furniture and are powered by batteries. This mixture of lighting can really add something else to the room, so mixing and matching them makes sense.

With the living room, you may have a favorite spot where you sit and read, so for this, hygge would essentially demand that you have a light near that spot that is not too bright, but also not too dim to allow you to do this. You should be able to reach the light in order to switch it on and off when required since the ease of access concept is also very important.

There is also the sense of the correct placement of lights elsewhere. Candles on the fireplace can add a certain sense of warmth and delicacy to the room, as well as providing that cozy feeling that you should be seeking. In addition, adding candles to the top of a table rather than a lamp, or having the ability to switch between the two, can also make a difference. You may also find that placing candles by the window for those dark evenings adds a healthy glow to the room that is both warm and inviting.

It is also an option for you to look at furniture and how it can be softly lit to brighten up those dark corners. Once again, you don't want to just have a lamp as an option as versatility and the ability to change the atmosphere is an important part, so you may wish to consider using lights that are battery powered and draping them over objects in order to bring light to those dark spaces. Doing that in various areas of the room can just add some life without it being overpowering, resulting in the perfect atmosphere.

Considerations for Other Rooms

Now we will move away from the living room for just a moment and consider the other rooms in the home and how different lighting can be used for various purposes.

The bathroom really should provide you with the opportunity to change the lighting depending on your needs. At times, brighter lights are clearly required for the sake of personal grooming, but even with this, there are ways in which you can alter your approach.

For the Danes, this could involve not using the bright overhead light, but rather having a mirror with lights around it so you can still see what you are doing. They will also try as much as possible to have a bathroom with a window to allow natural light to come in, which is no surprise considering the role it plays in hygge in general, as well as using candles. This will allow you to create a relaxing atmosphere in the bathroom.

The bedroom is another important room where lighting is going to be key. The Danes don't generally believe in using bright lights as the bedroom is a place to rest and be comfortable, and strong lighting doesn't tend to lend itself to that.

With this room, they will usually have small bedside lamps with a low wattage. You might want to take things further and use lamps that have various settings that alter the brightness. This provides you with the opportunity to change the light according to the atmosphere that you wish to create.

Even the kitchen is not exempt from this attempt at lighting and, yet again, there has to be some kind of balance between safety and providing atmosphere.

One thing that Danes do is have a main light as well as other, softer lights in darker corners. They may even apply lights underneath cupboards to shine down on worktops with these being softer in nature but just being enough to add a warm glow to the room.

The Conclusion on Lighting

The point we are making here is that the Danes believe in the power of light to do more than just allowing you to see in a room when it's dark outside. They believe that it has the ability to really change a room and set the scene, whether the goal is relaxing or entertaining.

What you must do is assess your lighting situation. Throw out the majority of those bright bulbs and lights that dominate, and replace them with light sources that are softer and more pleasant to sit around.

Chapter 7

Space in and Around the Home

Space in and around the home is yet another central point in hygge. However, modern-day living has made this seem almost like the impossible dream. In the Western world, we often live in smallish homes or apartments, and yet we try to own so many objects that our homes can sometimes resemble a storage unit rather than anything else.

Do yourself a huge favor and take a moment to walk into each room in your home and view it from the doorway. While you do this, look at how many items you have for the room. Do you feel as if the objects are lost in the vastness of the space? If you do, then you are fine, but there's a pretty good chance that this will not be the case for most people.

With this, we cannot forget about the space outside our homes either as we, once again, seem to have this amazing ability to accumulate 'things,' even if it's just for a patio area or a garden. How often do people end up thinking that their garden is disorganized and that they are unable to really enjoy it in the way they should? Once more, we see that this emotion is going against hygge, so we need to consider taking the concepts outdoors to the space that immediately surrounds our home.

Space is Relaxing

If you look at the typical Danish home, you will notice a lot of space in the various rooms. This often brings with it a sense of calm as no objects appear to be on top of one another, which is always difficult to deal with.

The Danes are content with what the room is laid out for, and they make sure that nothing gets in the way of that function. You should refer back to the idea of ease of access which we discussed in an earlier chapter, as it should all make sense when you think about the use of space.

You see, hygge is about being able to breathe and breathing becomes harder in a confined space. If you are in a room and there's no space, with objects dominating the walls and every surface, then it's not hygge.

It's important that you create a sense of ease in the room. Ease to move around. An ease to use the room in the way you intended it. An ease to come and go as you please. Your home should never be stressful to you in any way, and hygge allows you to work through each room and create the kind of space you want.

Space is Different for Everyone

Here is something that you cannot forget: space is different for everyone. We all have different ideas of what constitutes space for us, as some individuals feel comfortable with a more closed in feeling than others.

That's why we aren't setting you tasks of what you need to do for the sake of using hygge in your home, as it all rests on your shoulders.

However, we do feel that you should consider several points to help you along.

- Are you sure you understand the function of the space?
- Have you mastered the art of ease of access for those functions?
- Have you worked through the different objects and identified what should be kept?
- How does the atmosphere in the room feel compared to earlier?

The Danes love the idea of freshness in their lives. However, they also enjoy the cozy feeling, and hygge is a balance of both. Space plays a big role in this, and the Danes thoroughly enjoy the freedom that it gives in their home. Identify the space, work with the function you have in mind, and you will see that there is a new lease on life for each room in your home.

Chapter 8

Clutter and the Stress of Life and De-cluttering for Mindfulness

Clutter causes stress—there, we said it. It also makes us feel swamped with items and puts pressure on us to find some kind of place to store all of the objects that we accumulate through life.

Doing this is easier said than done, and so we find ourselves becoming even more stressed at that thought, and we enter into a downward spiral that resembles a cluttered abyss.

Hygge is anti-clutter.

Hygge hates clutter.

In actual fact, clutter is the complete opposite of hygge, and that's why there is so much of an emphasis on de-cluttering not only your home, but also your life. Because of this, you will feel refreshed and as if you have more space to breathe, which can never be a bad thing at all.

But how does one do it? How do you actually go about de-cluttering in accordance with the relatively rough guidelines as laid out by hygge? Well, the answer to that has to be, "in the least stressful way possible." At the root of this approach is the very idea of mindfulness.

Understanding Mindfulness for the Home

Mindfulness is all about being in the moment and allowing your mind to focus on the thing you are doing or experiencing at that time. It's about blocking out those external thoughts that allow our mind to race ahead and put our brain under even more stress.

Now, you might be wondering how on earth you are going to apply mindfulness to decluttering your home, but mindfulness uses some very basic concepts that are easy to take advantage of.

The first step is to not just start throwing things out; this would be crazy. While decluttering, you need to be in the moment. You cannot just get a garbage bag and start throwing things away. That's not what this is about. Instead, you have to refer back to the earlier chapters in this book that looked at objects and how to assess their need, importance, and meaning to you. By doing this, you can then peacefully ascertain if something should be kept or moved on to a new home.

Instead, you need to think about the points we have mentioned in previous chapters.

- What is the function?
- How easy is it to use this item?
- Do I have any attachment to the object?
- Is it obstructing me from using the room as I want?

The one thing that we don't want you to do is have regrets when it comes to decluttering your home. You must feel safe in the decisions you have made as to what stays and what goes, and that's why doing it at any time other than when you have a clear head is not acceptable.

Dealing with that Clutter

Remember the chapter where we spoke about giving items away? If not, then it's recommended that you go back and read it once more because it's important.

Just because an item is clutter in one room, does not have to mean that it is clutter in other rooms. It may be that it is just in the wrong location, so you need to think over the entire house rather than just the room you are dealing with.

That's another reason why you must do this when you are in the correct frame of mind. It's far too easy to make some mistakes, and then how will you feel when you realize this and it's too late to rescue the item in question?

This needs to be done methodically. You need to do one room at a time and understand why you are taking these actions. You must look at one object at a time and come to that decision as to whether or not it stays or goes.

Do a bit of the room, stand back, and see how you feel. Have the feelings that you have for the room improved, or is there still some work that needs to be done? It might take a few attempts for you to reach a point where you are content with the room.

Overall, clutter isn't bad—it's just annoying and weighs you down. Hygge is all about that freedom and only having the items that serve a purpose. Clutter tends to not serve any purpose once you get to a certain point. Do you really need those extra chairs that are never used? Are those ornaments serving a purpose other than gathering dust?

Be honest with yourself, as honesty is a good trait to have. If it won't have a negative impact on your life or enjoyment of the room or its purpose, then it could be classed as clutter. However, even after you have managed to throw out the items that you don't need, there's still the organizing to do, which is what we will move onto next.

Chapter 9

Organizing Each Room

As you may have guessed by now, organization is key. The difficulty is that we often have no idea where to even begin, so we then don't bother at all. This is hardly the correct way to go about it and practitioners of hygge would be horrified at that very idea.

But why do we take that approach? Why is being organized often so difficult or alien to us?

It is just a sign of the general chaos of our lives. We are so used to being surrounded by stress and anxiety that we will often bring it home with us, and that's not exactly helpful. However, there is a way to counteract this, and it involves you understanding how to organize your home and do so in a productive way.

The good news is that hygge sets out to directly tackle this issue. For the Danes, a disorganized room is a major faux pas, and you would be hard pressed to find a home in Denmark that is like that.

Look at it from this perspective. The idea of a home being organized with everything having its place is not just a Danish thing, but a Scandinavian approach in general. Why do you think that Ikea is all about clever storage ideas and straight lines? They are adopting those very same principles where the idea of clutter and things being strewn all over a room is just not allowed to happen.

So, as you would expect, there are a number of advantages associated with organizing a room and it's worthwhile checking them out to really allow this point to hit home.

The Advantages of Organization

If we can look more closely at what's going on when we organize, we can then begin to understand the various advantages.

First, it de-stresses you when you know where everything is. By knowing that every item has its place, you can find an object easily rather than rummaging around desperately trying to remember where you last put it. This alone fits in perfectly with the concept of hygge as the Danes are all about clever storage and placement of items, so they know where everything is in an instant.

Next, it lets you know what you have. If things aren't organized, then it stands to reason that you could be confused as to what you have and what you don't have. This ties in with the previous chapter regarding de-cluttering your home.

A third reason is that it saves you time. By being able to go to anything you want immediately, it stops you rummaging around and the frustration that always comes with that action. You stay calmer and more at ease with yourself when you know where those car keys are going to be, or your phone, or anything else that springs to mind.

So, how do you do it? How do you go about organizing things in accordance with the concept of hygge? Well, if we are honest, there's nothing special about it, and the vast majority is just going to be common sense on your part.

An Example of Organization

To really stress the approach that you need to take, we can look at a room in your home as an example. In this instance, we will think about the kitchen as this really does tend to be the heart of the home for most families. Also, the kitchen can tend to be rather cluttered with things crammed into cupboards haphazardly.

So, this is what you would do if you were adopting the principles of hygge. Now, to make life a bit easier, we are going to assume that you have already done the de-cluttering step and thrown out various items so you are left with those pieces that you really want to keep. So, at this point, you then know exactly what you have to organize.

Step 1: Understanding Space

The first thing is to understand how much space you have available for storing things. How on earth are you going to be able to sort things out if you have no concept of where items can go or how to deal with it?

Now, this isn't about measuring space or being aware of the size of your cupboards, but you need to gain an understanding of the layout, where the space is, and also the flow of the kitchen before you move forward.

Step 2: The Flow

The flow is important. The best organization is where items are kept in a logical manner so you can get to them and are not crossing a room or reaching up for one thing and then down low for another. Doing this is stressful and, as you know, stress is something that is frowned upon in hygge.

This is why it's so important that you de-clutter first and immediately prior to trying to organize things. It lets you know the items you have and from that, you can begin to work out the order with the flow in mind.

Step 3: Grouping Things Together

One thing that the Danes are very good at is making sure that items that are supposed to go together are actually kept together. This just makes so much sense, and you may even be sitting there wondering why on earth it has been mentioned. Surely everyone does this?

Well, you would be surprised to discover that this isn't the case. In fact, most of us are guilty of starting off with things being organized, only for that organization to slide due to us being lazy, not having the time, and a multitude of other reasons.

Let's think of another, simpler example.

In your living room, you probably have a number of different electrical items that come with a remote control of some kind. Now, how do you organize them? How often do you find yourself searching for one of the controls, only to discover that it is in some strange part of the room?

For those that are focused on adopting hygge into their home, they will look at something as simple as the remote control issue and seek to resolve the problem before it can even occur.

With this, they would look at having a remote control holder, one that's large enough to hold every control in the room. The holder would be in a prominent and easily accessible spot and after it had been used, the control would be placed back there, ready for the next time.

You have to admit that this sounds so much easier than controls being scattered to all four corners of the room. You know where each one is and you know where to look when you want to use it. How much easier can it get?

In this instance, you need to look at each room and ascertain which items deserve to go together, whether it be for storage or with how they are going to be used. By doing this, you will then find order in your home, and this will bring those stress levels down.

Chapter 10

Bringing the Outside In

A huge part of hygge is connected to the concept of bringing the outside in. To better understand this, you can look at Scandinavian interior design ideas and see how the natural elements are loved and adored in pretty much every room. We did, of course, speak about the importance of light in a previous chapter, so in this instance we aren't talking about that, but there's still a lot for us to get through.

In Danish homes, there is often a sense of a general flow between the outdoors and indoors. The two seem to work together seamlessly and this in itself creates a certain sense of calm and order in each room. This is an approach that you are strongly advised to take and we will discuss the benefits of it later in the chapter.

It's no surprise to find out that the Danes love to use natural textures and materials in their home and this has been long known for its ability to relax a room.

Dealing with Materials

One thing that you will often find in Danish homes is that they use natural textures and wood in their interiors. It seems to bring a certain sense of peace and calm that you have included nature in your home and the beauty that it can offer.

Also, there's never any need for them to overdo these natural materials. The very idea of having a room swathed in wood would be seen as horrific as it can often be rather impersonal if you rely too heavily on it.

What we are talking about here are things that include the following:

- Window blinds can be in natural material.

- Chair coverings can be in a natural material.
- The same can be applied to cushions.
- Other soft furnishings can also be included.

It's More Than Just Textures

But there's more to it than using natural textures. Instead, by using wood and even including plants placed in strategic locations, you are effectively bringing some life into a room and that, in its own self, is a key part of hygge.

Think of the way in which a vase full of fresh flowers can not only bring a sense of beauty to a room, but also the way that the aroma can fill the air. It brings a sense of freshness not only to the spot where the vase is placed, but the entire room.

In fact, this is a wonderful example of how something so simple can completely change the atmosphere of the room and that's something we have been working on throughout the course of this book. Of course, there is then the need to keep changing the flowers once they are past their best as having something that is either dead or dying is certainly not a pleasurable experience.

At the same time, if you are fortunate enough to have a window that looks out onto some kind of view, even if it is of your garden, then take advantage of it. Avoid cluttering up the window obstructing your view and allow it to become a vista that you can be proud of and enjoy. Being able to look out of the window and take pleasure from what you see is a wonderful thing.

By rights, you should find that your mind is racing as to what you could use in each room, but don't put yourself under pressure to include nature all over the home. Instead, it may be appropriate to have just slight glimpses rather than it being a dominant feature, but this really does vary according to so many other factors.

Cool Tips to Help with Nature and Hygge

Finally, let's look at some rather cool tips on how you can combine nature and hygge in and around your home. Remember, you can often do all of this on a budget, so drop the idea that it has to cost you a fortune. That is really not the case at all.

1. Consider growing plants in the kitchen.

It makes sense to look at growing some herbs indoors in the kitchen. Not only is it useful, but the act of growing the herbs and then using them in your own cooking is hygge encapsulated. Have a corner or a spot next to a window with a lot of natural light and effectively turn it into a small, indoor garden.

2. Potted plants in other rooms can help.

Potted plants can be used in more places than you expect. However, one tip is to have something fresh and alive in the hallway, if possible, as it gives a pleasant feeling when you walk into the home. As we said, the bathroom can often be spruced up by some kind of plant in the corner, but it shouldn't be the dominant feature.

3. Splashes of nature make a bigger impact.

You want any object or feature to stand out from everything else. Due to this, you need to think about using just splashes of nature rather than it being something that dominates the room. This can be sensory overload, and who wants that?

4. Never allow anything to die.

Something that is broken or damaged in some way is not following hygge. So, if flowers or plants are past their best, replace them immediately. Something that is alive and pleasant to look at lifts the spirits at different times, so it makes sense that the opposite would also apply at most times.

Do yourself a favor and look at helping to bring the outside into your home. It is known that being in touch with nature has a calming effect on the mind and soul, so it's perhaps no surprise that it is seen as being a useful tool when it comes to hygge. Also, look at some images of Danish homes and see how they incorporate it into their own particular style as inspiration. However, just add your very own touch rather than doing a carbon copy.

Chapter 11

Bringing Peace to the Home via Decorating

Once you have removed the clutter and started to introduce the outdoors and nature into your home, we have to offer some guidance on how to decorate your home to then bring more peace to the atmosphere. Remember that peace and serenity are important in hygge and something that should start to weave their magic from the moment you walk through the door.

Now, obviously, every individual will have their own personal tastes when it comes to the décor in their home, but a few general ideas may help to guide you in the right direction. However, do remember that one of the beautiful things about hygge is the way in which you are free to express yourself and do what makes you happy and feel comfortable, so there are no real rules to concern yourself with.

But, how exactly do you bring peace to the home and enjoy a more relaxing atmosphere? Well, it's a lot easier than you may have been fearing.

We aren't really talking about full-on changes here. Instead, subtlety is often the key and it's how you use those little changes that really is important.

We are going to assume that you have already carried out all of those chores about functionality and organizing and that you are ready to add decorative touches that can make a real difference.

Decorating the Hygge Way

One of the cool things about decorating in this manner is that you can really get involved in the process. Remember, hygge has the habit of incorporating mindfulness and takes advantage of its calming thoughts and this can be extended to decorating.

In Denmark, as well as other Scandinavian countries that include hygge as a way of life, decorating a home is a wonderful thing to do. The family gets involved in the process to make sure that the tastes and interests of everybody that is affected by each room have been taken into account.

There are no limits in what you can do, so why should your imagination be restricted in this manner?

With hygge, you need to immerse yourself in the action of decorating. There is a strong sense of needing to be involved in the thoughts of what each paint color, or flooring option, or window dressing actually means to you.

When decorating, you need to feel that everything is coming together. That you love each item you have used or that your color scheme is exactly what you want. There is no real concept of trying to make do with what you have, that's not hygge. Instead, there has to be a sense of contentment and accomplishment when a room has been decorated. By doing so, you will have a greater sense of comfort in that room.

Also, if you feel that you are too busy to decorate a room on your own and wish to hire a professional, we recommend that you don't do this. Make time even to do one wall or change one thing at a time. Change can be gradual, as hygge and decorating a home is not meant to be rushed. You get no prize for painting an entire room in a matter of hours. In fact, this is something that should be avoided.

It's Not About the Colors

With decorating, or interior design in general, we are often told what is in vogue at any given time and there is a sense of pressure to adopt those styles or colors in our own home.

Well, if this is something that you do, then stop it immediately.

Hygge, as you must be aware of by now, is all about a sense of freedom. It's about being in your own space, and do you know what comes with that? Choosing the colors or textures that you want to have. To choose the things that bring you pleasure over and above anything else.

If you find that having bright green brings you pleasure, then go for it. Never allow some designer to tell you that it's not in fashion. Who are they to actually tell you this when you personally love it?

If you like that crazy looking sofa, then have it if it brings you a sense of happiness every single time you either look at it or sit on it. After all, that's what this is all about—having a sense of joy in your home. The décor is a huge part of that.

Now, we aren't saying that you cannot look for inspiration. In fact, this is a wonderful way to find out what actually makes you happy as you could be surprised at the answers you get.

The main thing is that the Danes will seek that inspiration and then put their own style or twist to it so that it becomes their own. They don't just look in a magazine or on the Internet and copy what they see. That would only be done in exceptional circumstances where everything was the exact same, but what are the chances of that happening?

Remember the Small Things

Okay, so painting the walls or changing the flooring in some way are huge decorating jobs, but the small changes can often bring you the most pleasure, and yet they tend to be overlooked.

Take that small table that sits there and looking out of place. With this, you have a choice to make. You can donate it, or there's also the opportunity to re-purpose it and give the table a new lease on life.

For this, you would need to take the rest of what you were doing in the room into consideration, as that determines the colors or the end look. Of course, you can do this with just about anything, so do see this as a possibility rather than just assuming that an item cannot fit into a room because the walls are now a different shade.

In addition, you need to keep in mind those small changes and finishing touches that can make a real difference to the way in which you view the room. Those beautiful lamps that give off the perfect glow. That comfortable chair positioned near the fireplace with a reading lamp nearby. The luxurious rug in the middle of the floor that feels so snug when you put your bare feet on it.

This all adds up, but you need to keep in the forefront of your mind that practicality, warmth, and a use for the room will always be key. Also, stop adding clutter to the room as you have worked hard to get rid of it. By all means decorate with a few small pieces, but never overdo it or you run the very real risk of destroying all of the hard work you have carried out.

This is what we recommend that you do when you are looking at trying to replicate that amazing hygge atmosphere.

- Never rush into decorating; take your time with your decisions.
- Choose colors or materials that you like, no matter what they are.
- Become immersed in the decorating process at all times.
- Create your own style, although do look for inspiration elsewhere.
- Remember the reason for the space and how the décor can reflect that reason.

As you can see, there's nothing too complex here, and yet, it's amazing how often people will make a mess of things when it comes to decorating their home. In the end, you want each room to have its own character and that it fits in with what the room is used for. Purpose is everything and the decorating aspect is not immune to that.

Chapter 12

Useful Tips for Each Room in the Home

Understandably, we have covered a lot throughout the book up until this point, but it may still be the case that you are sitting there wondering where you even begin with each room in your home.

It's impossible to offer a completely fool-proof guide for what you should do in each room because we simply have no idea how many rooms you have, what the light situation is like, what limitations you have, and so on.

Keeping that in mind, there are still a number of tips that you may find useful when they are applied to each room. Clearly, if you do not have something that is described, then you may be tempted to skip on by, but that would be a shame. After all, there may be tips in those sections that appeal to you and could be used elsewhere in your home.

The Entrance Hallway

Often, we clutter the entrance hallway with shoes and coats hanging on the wall, but we aren't telling you to put everything away so that the hallway is empty of them.

Instead, choose just one main coat for the season and have that hanging. Cut back on the number of shoes that are sitting there and have a nice shoe rack so they are organized and in their place. Another great touch, which is really Danish, is to have a basket with gloves for you going out, or warm and thick socks for when you come home. It's a little, comforting item that can have such a positive effect on your mind and soul.

Make sure the lighting in the hallway is warm and welcoming, as well. It makes your home look more inviting.

The Living Room

The living room will tend to be one of the most widely used rooms in the home, so it's important that you understand how to dress it correctly when trying to incorporate hygge into your life.

Begin by throwing out those powerful lights and swap them for a lower wattage bulb. Add some warmth with throws, thick rugs, comfortable cushions, and various candle holders dotted around the room. Identify dark areas and use small lights or even fairy lights to add some warmth to them.

Make sure each item in the lounge has some kind of purpose. Have chairs as comfortable as possible. Allow light to enter the room via the window. Allow air to circulate to create a freshness in the room. Consider using white furniture or throw blankets to allow the light to bounce off the surfaces and make everything seem even brighter than before.

The Kitchen

With hygge, there is no doubt that the kitchen is indeed the heart of the home. If you have a dining space included here, then you are onto a real winner.

Once again, you need to allow as much light into the room as possible. Also, keep fresh fruit and vegetables on view since this is effectively bringing some form of life to the kitchen. Include wooden chopping boards and wooden worktops with light cupboards. Have a number of cupboards with glass fronts allowing you to add lights to the inside since this adds a different atmosphere to the room. Use small lights underneath cupboards to light the worktop rather than have the room dominated by one single large ceiling light.

If you do have a dining table here, then make sure it is always ready to welcome any guests that may pop in for a chat. It needs to be accessible, take minutes to set, and it should not be crammed into a corner. There should be a sense of freedom surrounding it so that individuals would want to sit there for what would feel like hours chatting, eating, and generally having fun together.

The Bathroom

The bathroom is clearly a functional space, but that doesn't mean you need to forget the décor and taking advantage of hygge. It's certainly a case of you being able to adapt the room for whatever kind of atmosphere you are seeking at the time. After all, a bathroom should be capable of becoming a space where you are able to pamper yourself, so there's a need for your décor to allow you to switch lights.

With this, we aren't just talking about candlelight, either. Try lights surrounding the main bathroom mirror that will illuminate the room without taking over. Consider plants in the room, if possible, and to have fresh towels. Make sure that there is a towel heating radiator so that you can enjoy that feeling of the warm towel after a shower.

If you are a lover of various pampering products, then always check you have adequate storage and can access everything easily. The one thing that you simply cannot do is to have all of those bottles scattered around in a haphazard way. It's messy, it's chaotic, and it's certainly not hygge.

The Bedroom

This applies no matter if we are talking about the master bedroom or a guest bedroom, as the same principles apply at all times.

The bedroom is a place for rest and reflection, and that is something that hygge and the Danes are experts at doing in their own home. Too often, people will have television sets, their smartphones, laptops, and various other electrical gadgets that effectively take you away from the main idea behind the room even existing in the first place.

It's no surprise to find out that we are talking about the need for mood lighting here, but also perhaps a chair in the corner of the room by the window where you can read or sit back and listen to music in order to relax.

You see, even though we are talking about removing electronic gadgets from the room, we aren't talking about the bedroom becoming solely a place for sleep—far from it.

You should be able to turn it into a kind of haven. Once again, natural light should flood in as much as possible and bedding should be of the best quality that you can afford.

Your bedroom should feel luxurious and comfortable at all times. You should be able to feel snug and cozy whenever you go in there. Most importantly, it should clearly be a place to rest and effectively close the door to all of the stresses in the world. Oh, and using mirrors to bounce the natural light around the room is also a very good idea.

The reason for this chapter has been to try and provide you with a sense of the few things that you can do in order to change a room when it comes to the décor. Of course, we do recommend that you also incorporate the other points that have been raised in the earlier chapters, as it's best when this works as a whole.

Chapter 13

Summing Things Up

This final chapter will summarize the things we learned about hygge and give you a confidence boost for your task of bringing hygge to your home. To be honest, there's not really a right or wrong way to use hygge, since we are all different and what brings us comfort will vary from person to person.

Perhaps the main idea that you need to take from this book is that adopting hygge should be done with a certain air of calmness. Getting frustrated, annoyed, depressed, or anything negative goes directly against the concept of hygge.

Take your time with this. It is a peaceful process that is done at your own leisure with an acceptance that each small change that you make is going to have a profound impact on the serenity that you feel in your home.

The Danes hate clutter. They also hate things not having a purpose or being in the wrong place. As we said earlier, this kind of chaos is often regarded as being representative of your chaotic approach to life, and that's not a good thing. They prefer to walk into their home and to be met with a real sense of things being the way that they should. Nothing is out of place, and the atmosphere and general feeling in the home is relaxing. It allows them to perhaps forget about the stresses and issues that affect the world outside and when they close that door, they can enter into this wonderful world where everything is as it should be.

You have to admit that this sounds like our very own sense of utopia, and perhaps that's what you should be seeking.

Throughout this book, we have been looking at providing you with some ideas that you can perhaps apply, but you will have hopefully noticed that there have been no set rules to abide by. The reason for that is simple: we just wanted to guide you through things rather than instruct you on exactly what to do. This in itself is a good example of hygge, as it's about what makes you happy and relaxed and who else, apart from yourself, can understand what it is that affects you in this way?

So, how would we sum up what you should do in order to give your home that Danish feel and to embrace hygge? Well, for us there are several things that stand out from everything else, and if you can apply your own version of these ideas, then you will create a wonderful space to be enjoyed not only by yourself, but also by anybody who visits.

1. Understand what you like.

When we talk about understanding what you like, we really mean for you to come to terms with the kind of things that help you feel peaceful. What de-stresses you in the home? What brings you joy? What irritates and annoys you and should, therefore, be avoided?

There is absolutely no chance of you being able to adopt these Danish principles if you have no concept of what it is that makes you tick. Failure to do this means you are going to fail in your entire approach.

2. Understand what you own.

We spoke extensively about objects as it is those items that we own that will lead to the biggest problems when trying to adopt these principles of hygge and make your home more peaceful than it is at the current time.

How often do you go through a cupboard and find things that you had completely forgotten about? if you find yourself saying 'oh I forgot all about that,' then you need to ask yourself the question, was it really that important to you? Generally, if you forgot that it existed, then it can't have played a big role in your life.

3. Be prepared to throw items out.

We generally have too much clutter and as we have said in earlier chapters, clutter brings stress. Also, clutter makes it harder for anything to have order and, according to hygge and the Danes, having order is of the utmost importance.

To be honest, you must be ready to be quite brutal when going through your objects, but at the same time, there's a need for you to work through your belongings with a clear mind and with an end goal to aim for.

Furthermore, it was mentioned that you need to let objects go with a happy heart. You should be content to look at them and realize that they have served their purpose and it's now the correct time for them to be enjoyed by others. That's why donating them either to someone you know or to a charity shop is such a fulfilling thing to do and it is strongly encouraged.

4. Be aware of your space.

Space is important in hygge and Danish homes. We aren't even talking about there being a need to live in a home with vast rooms. Instead, as the Danes are not big on being outlandish, they tend to live in relatively modest homes, and yet they can make the space on the inside appear much bigger than it really is.

This is all about making the best of what you have at your disposal. It's about putting thought into taking advantage of each part of a room, and the space surrounding you always having its purpose.

In fact, we spoke about the need for you to understand the purpose of each spot and for your rooms to often be multi-functional and able to switch their purpose depending on your needs at the time. This can only be done when you have a full awareness of the space itself.

5. Keep an eye on your décor.

Décor can really make or break a room and this is especially true when you are looking at using hygge in your home. Now, it's easy enough to go ahead and study the Scandinavian styles as they are pretty well known, but at the end of the day, it's all about what makes you happy and content.

However, we do strongly recommend that you are aware of the need to create that cozy atmosphere whether it's achieved by soft lighting, candles, warm throws, fluffy rugs, or anything else that can create that feeling. It's something that you should do in each room and even leading up to the door to your home, if this is possible, as hygge starts from the moment you approach your home.

6. Remember the outside and nature.

Finally, nature and the outdoors are very important in hygge. The Danes love to bring the outside to the inside as it adds freshness to the place and it creates a special connection with the natural world.

We mentioned how you should be looking at natural textures and items in your home as well as plants, but please don't forget the idea of bringing as much natural light as possible into your home, as that will make a huge difference. Avoid cluttering the window or having anything that can obstruct it because the darkness can lead to you feeling more depressed.

Overall, we strongly recommend that you try to have some fun when adding a touch of hygge and the Danish way of life to your home. Anybody can achieve it and you don't even have to spend a fortune in order to do so, and this alone is a huge bonus. Small changes in each room can have a large impact on how you feel in any given space.

This can be a real voyage of discovery for you. It allows you to look at your home from a completely different perspective, one that will bring you a sense of comfort and peace of mind. There is no right, and there is no wrong in hygge. It all depends on your own personal tastes and needs rather than obeying a set of rules that have been laid down by somebody else.

Look at your home and make a plan. Make that plan to organize, de-clutter, and give your home a purpose. Breathe new life into it and you will then find greater enjoyment than you ever thought possible.

Now, does that not sound like a better approach to your home? Does that not sound like something that you would like to go ahead and do?

You bet it does, so get to it!

I put a lot of hard work and effort into my books and I love to know what you my reader thinks about it.

If you could leave an honest review for this book, only a sentence or two to let me know your thoughts. I read all of the reviews and use them to help improve my books.

Part 2: Hygge Living

The Practical Guide To Creating a Simple & Cozy Lifestyle The Danish Way

Introduction: Peaceful, Cozy Living

How does the prospect of having a peaceful life sound? To many, this is the ideal way to live, and yet it appears to be so far out of our reach that we believe that it is unattainable.

Instead of peace, we find ourselves consumed with the frenetic pace of modern life. We allow ourselves to be caught up in social media, obsessed with our to-do lists, stuck in traffic on a constant basis, and then when we get home, we just want to collapse in bed. The worst part is having to repeat the same process the following day.

This is hardly peaceful.

But it doesn't have to be that way. Instead, we can turn to the Danish way of life and learn from their habits and the ways in which they bring a sense of cozy and comfortable living that is largely free from the stresses and strains that we tend to place upon ourselves. It's a way of life that results in you making your life relatively simple in order to enjoy the things around you.

This way of life is called *hygge*.

Throughout this book, we are going to explore not only the origins of the hygge way of life, but also the different areas of your existence into which it can be incorporated. We will spend time examining your own self as well as your home to help you create that sense of peace and calm that you have been desperately searching for. We will also go further and look at how hygge can be applied to your experiences, friends, relationships, and even your work. By doing so, you will learn how to feel more fulfilled and content with each and every aspect of your life.

Denmark is regarded as being the happiest nation in the world, and hygge is the most important aspect that Danes attribute this to. If that is the case, then attempting to incorporate it into your own life takes on even more importance.

We are not talking about wholesale changes. Often, subtle differences can have a huge and positive impact. By the end, you will not view your life as being completely different. Instead, you will view it with a new sense of contentment that had undoubtedly been missing before.

So, let us start to change your life.

Chapter 1

The Origins of Hygge and its Meaning

We can begin our journey by offering an explanation of the origins of hygge. The word itself is one that you may not have heard of up until this point, and there is no literal translation that we can offer you.

Instead, it is generally accepted that hygge is more of a feeling or thought. It is connected to the idea of cozy and comfortable living. It's something that brings peace to both your heart and mind.

To some, hygge may appear to be a fantasy world as the idea of having a life such as this is an alien concept that is impossible to achieve. Even, if that is what you believe, this book will still be for you.

Although it is the Danes who have really transformed this concept into an art form, to get to the absolute root of the movement we have to jump to another Scandinavian country, Norway. However, this is a bit of a cheat, if we are honest, as the first appearance of the theory of hygge came at a time when Denmark and Norway had a close bond. Indeed, they shared so many aspects that they were practically the same country, only the names were different.

In fact, even though we will refer to the Danes repeatedly through this book, the term hyggé only appeared in the Danish language and literature approximately 150 years ago. However, it is fair to say that they have since taken the concept and made it their own. Indeed, they are now regarded as being the main exporters of hygge.

Also, Denmark is not the only country that uses the concepts that we will take you through during this e-book. Instead, Scandinavian countries as a whole have applied the same rules and approaches, and even Germany has its own version, just with slight changes in the language. However, no matter the country you are in, there are various aspects of hygge that can be applied to any circumstances or situations. It certainly is adaptable to anything that you wish to throw at it.

Of course, it is difficult for us to really understand why it took off in popularity. Denmark is often a dark and cold country, and at times it can be tough to understand how you could find anything that is cozy or comfortable in such a climate.

But then, perhaps that is also the reason as to why hygge became so entrenched in the minds of the Danes. Perhaps it was all down to the fact that they were forced to look inward to find peace and serenity because the outside world made it so difficult? That is a question that is just to be pondered, but at the same time it generates some interesting possibilities.

If that is indeed the case, then they have successfully developed a way of life that has had a profound impact on not only the Danes themselves but those individuals around the world that have also embraced the concept. Hygge has brought peace to the world. Hygge has brought some sense of stability and safety during a time when people are feeling more frenetic than ever.

Looking at the Concept in More Depth

From its relatively scant beginnings, hygge has become something of a buzzword in recent years, but it would be wrong for us to look at it from that particular perspective. After all, if it has been used in a productive manner for well over a century, then is it actually a buzz term? The answer is a resounding *no*.

There can be little doubt that hygge is certainly taking the world by storm as we all seek that sense of peace and calmness in our lives and to feel comfortable as much as possible. Often, we see this as an impossibility, and yet hygge has opened up the very real possibility of this now becoming something we can achieve. The best part is that it is so easy to incorporate different aspects of this hygge movement into your life.

The problem, and it is something we will look at throughout this book, is that people often attribute hygge to just the home. This is wrong. Instead, the concept can be applied to each and every part of life from the things we own, to how we live in our homes. Our friends and relationships can undergo the same processes, as can our professional lives. Indeed, you can turn attention to your own self and start from deep inside when you are considering adopting these strategies. After all, change has to always come from you and nowhere else.

The Danes see each and every part as being a piece of the jigsaw puzzle that is life. In order to then have the complete picture, it is important that each piece fits in without any problems. If one piece is wrong, then the rest can become unbalanced.

That is not hygge.

You will learn how, right from the introduction of hygge, it is all about getting some order to your life and working past the chaos that surrounds us. Its very origins state how it can be the smaller things in life that often bring the most pleasure and contentment. A room lit only by candles. A roaring log fire in the cold winter months. A comfortable throw. Anything that brings peace to both your heart and mind.

The hardest part is to know where to even begin. You have probably surrounded yourself with events, friends, and belongings that, if truth be told, you aren't even sure if you want. However, we tend to hold onto things for that rainy day that never really happens. As a result, we become weighed down by all of these things that are just pointless.

This is also not hygge.

So, we need to work through this, and do so step by step. Don't worry, and don't freak out at this idea because it is going to be less uncomfortable than you might expect.

In order to do this, we have to go right back to basics. We need to look at what the aim is when it comes to the mind and hygge. Remember, the sense of being comfortable and happy in your surroundings starts in the mind. It is about being in the moment and enjoying what is around you and appreciating it for what it's worth.

That, ladies and gentlemen, is the art of mindfulness, and that is where we are going to begin the entire story of hygge.

Chapter 2

Understanding the Art of Mindfulness

In this chapter, we will explore a key component to the entire concept of hygge—the art of mindfulness.

To many, this is difficult to do. Being mindful is all about being in the moment. Focusing your mind on what you are doing, where you are, and not allowing yourself to be distracted by erroneous thoughts that are disruptive as well as destructive.

The problem is that often our minds are too busy. We have far too many things to think about, so everything becomes a haze and we can feel as if we are completely losing control. Hygge is all about regaining that control and bringing a sense of serenity to our minds.

Stress, anxiety, and depression are major concerns in the Western world. Research has shown that these issues are often linked to the pressures that we place ourselves under, so it's no surprise when various illnesses start to take hold as our bodies just cannot cope. So much of this can be undone if more people seek to include the concept of hygge and its more mindful approach to each and every aspect of our lives.

How Mindfulness Works in Accordance with Hygge

To perhaps better understand this, we need to make sure that we look at how mindfulness works in accordance with the principles of hygge. We covered the key aspects of hygge when examining its origins, so it's best if you can refresh your memory if required.

With mindfulness, there is an image that shows it in action using the difference between humans and animals. In the image, an individual is walking their dog. The individual has a thought bubble coming from their head, and it is full of noise and is chaotic. On the other hand, the dog has a thought bubble. Its bubble has an image, and that image is the scene it sees before it, the bit of grass, or whatever its surroundings may be.

The way in which the human and the dog approach the moment that they are in is vastly different. The human being is tense and rigid in their body language. They are stressed, and their mind is going at the speed of sound. They look exhausted.

The dog is relaxed. It is in the moment. It is connected to nature and is not stressed. It walks easily on the leash, and yet if the human was on the leash instead, then he would be pulling on it and growling at other humans that walk by.

It's hardly a cozy and comfortable way of living.

In a hygge world, there needs to be a sense of appreciation of everything that we have in our lives. We need to look at each object, moment, or individual that we encounter and be aware of what it, or they, can do for us.

Hygge, Mindfulness, and the Mind in General

Just prior to moving onto the next chapter where we get into the main concepts of hygge, it is useful to look at what is going on in the mind. The idea of hygge is that it de-stresses you. It relaxes you and makes you feel far more comfortable in not only body and mind, but also in your life in general.

Mindfulness does the exact same thing, and that is why the two are inextricably linked. It's no surprise that mindfulness is used as a way to reduce your stress levels as it slows down the adrenaline and instead forces your body into releasing more pleasurable and calming hormones.

This is getting too far into biology, but it does give you a sense of what you are hoping to achieve with hygge. You are hoping to achieve that point where you look at everything you own and appreciate it. You love and cherish each object as it brings you pleasure in some way.

With each object, you should look at it and study it. Work out what it is about its appearance or use that you enjoy. There is a sense of almost giving it some thanks and gratitude for being in your life and helping you.

Now, it might be no surprise to discover that you could want an example of how this all works, as it can be slightly confusing.

Take an armchair, for example. Look at the cushions and think about how comfortable they are. The back of the armchair is very supportive to your spine, and this further adds to the comfort levels. You love the color of it, the fabric, the shape of the legs. More importantly, it allows you to rest.

By looking at the chair and being content with it sitting there in your room, you are in the moment with that object. You are not allowing external thoughts and stresses to permeate your mind. The world, for that moment, comes across as a far more peaceful and pleasant place to be.

How to Incorporate Mindfulness and Hygge into Your Life

It is somewhat understandable if you now find yourself in the position whereby you are unsure as to how to incorporate this concept of mindfulness and hygge into your life. That is absolutely normal when something is new.

However, the task at hand is far simpler than you may be aware. Indeed, we are only looking at making a few changes to how you approach things. A few small changes can yield a huge difference.

Step 1: Finding the Time

The first step is to look at finding some spare time to really get to grips with mindfulness, and also your life in general. You would be amazed at how often it is that we don't do this as we are consumed by all of these external pressures that are placed upon us.

Well, if you are going to get anywhere with hygge, then you must make some space in your schedule or you will just go around in a stressful circle. We aren't even talking about hours at a time, either. You simply need to be willing to stop, rest, and take stock of your life and everything that's in it.

Do yourself a favor. When you finish work, or put the kids to bed, find a quiet spot and contemplate.

Step 2: Understanding What to Think About

Of course, you may find yourself becoming rather confused as to what you should think about, so let us help you.

Think of your life in general. Does it bring you pleasure, or are you stressed on a constant basis? If you are stressed, then why?

Look at your home and everything that you have in your possession. Consider how things make you feel and whether or not you are even able to enjoy what you own. If not, then we will help you with this later on because this is a big part of what hygge is all about.

You should also think about what, in general, makes you happy, and decide if you have those things in your life at this moment. Throw out all of those stressful thoughts as they are not doing you any good whatsoever.

Step 3: Becoming Mindful

This may very well be the hardest step for most people, especially when they are completely new to the concept of mindfulness. Trying to become mindful takes time as it is something that you must get used to. The reason why it can be so difficult is simply because our minds are trained to think about so many things at one time—but that is part of the problem.

Our minds will often search for so many to think about and deal with that it gets to the point where we get nothing done and only end up with a headache from overthinking things What to make for dinner or whether the laundry needs to be done are important tasks, but we can spend too much time thinking about them. Instead of dwelling on a never-ending to-do list, it's important to acknowledge that these tasks will be performed. You can take a minute to plan your day: put a load of laundry on before dinner and it will be ready once dinner is finished. Then, move your focus elsewhere. If you can organize your thoughts, you can find more time to be aware of the life around you.

In order to become mindful, one has to work at blocking out any intrusive thoughts from entering the mind. They only stress us out and serve no purpose at all. This does take some work, but here are some ways to start the process:

- Look at the room you are in at this moment in time.
- Take a moment to observe what is around you and what each object means.
- Have no distractions.
- Have peace and quiet surrounding you.
- Allow yourself to effectively daydream about an object or place all on its own.

By doing this, you will begin to experience a new sense of relaxation and calm. These are the feelings that hygge tries to bring into your life. Looking inward in your life and making the changes that are required will not only improve your quality of life, but also will reduce your stress levels in general.

Clearly, there is some work to do, and being aware of losing yourself in the moment, object, or experience is not even the main part of hygge. Instead, we need to look more closely at those various aspects of your life, and we will start with where it all begins for everyone—the home.

Chapter 3

Bringing Hygge into the Home

One of the key areas of hygge and the part of our life where so much of it can be implemented is the home. The home is the space we return to after a stressful day. It is the place where we rest and recharge our batteries for the day that is to follow. It is the place where we enjoy our family and friends.

It is the place where we wish to feel relaxed and able to just kick back and unwind.

Of course, the problem is that this is often not the case. Often, our home is chaotic and unpleasant no matter how hard we try. Clearly, most people are doing something wrong, and the thing that they are doing wrong is not grasping the idea of hygge. By making some alterations, you will bring a sense of order into your home life that has been sadly lacking. Things will suddenly have their place and purpose rather than simply collecting dust.

As a result, your home will become a place that you are happy to return to.

We aren't talking about making massive changes. It's not as if you will be stripping your home back to the absolute bare bones and starting all over. Instead, this is about making small changes that are then able to have a major impact on how you feel about the space as a whole. In order to do this, we need to begin by looking at key areas that are often a concern so you are then in a position to tackle them accordingly.

Also, it should be noted that this is something that everyone can do, and it also applies to each and every room of the home as well as the outside. In fact, anything that is seen as being your space, your part of the world, can be influenced by the concept of hygge. You just need to be willing to embrace the concept and put different things into action.

So, let us start things off with something that may not be that easy for some individuals.

Step 1: Assessing Your Belongings

Most people could be classed as being materialistic in some way. You might not even be aware of it, but over time we tend to have this innate ability to just accumulate 'stuff.' Materialism is anti-hygge. The accumulation of items and belongings just for the sake of owning something is not an accepted way of life in Denmark or other countries that embrace hygge.

- **List Your Spaces**

Start by walking through your house with a piece of paper and a pen. This is an arduous task that will take a lot of time. It's important to be thorough in order for minimalism to stick. As you walk around, both inside and out, take note of all your different spaces. Be specific. Don't just write bedroom. Instead, write bedroom and closet as two separate spaces. Similarly, in your kitchen, you can sperate into cupboards, counters, and pantry. Continue until you have a list of everywhere in your house. This list will seem daunting, but creating small, attainable goals will help in the process.

- **Decide on a Schedule**

Organizing schedules should have some structure but they should not be too rigid. Often you will find that it takes longer to go through items than you would have initially thought. As well, normal life is also happening. Children need to be taken to school, Dinner needs to be made, and Social events need to be attended.

Be realistic when deciding when you will look at each space. Maybe choose one room per week. Or, if you have a long weekend coming up, devote one whole day to organizing. You know how efficient you can be, and you won't change overnight just to accomplish this new task.

If you are honest, you will look around at your belongings, go into cupboards and other storage places, and then try to remember why you bought something, and even where or when. Also, how many times have you gone looking for something only to stumble across an item that you forgot that you owned? This all happens because we tend to collect too many things, so we have no idea how to deal with them or even why they exist.

So, the first thing that you need to do to successfully incorporate hygge into your home is to assess your belongings. You need to be honest with yourself, and even be quite brutal in deciding what to keep and what to throw out. This is the concept of de-cluttering your home, and we will revisit it once again later in this chapter.

This assessment may take you some time to complete, but you have to work through it as it forms the basis of hygge in the home. It gives you the canvas that you are then going to work from and produce a home that is far more relaxing and comfortable than it is at this moment in time.

At this point, it is all about the awareness of what you own. After that, you can then move onto the next step, which is bringing some sense of order to your home.

Step 2: Order and Practicality

Owning items, whether they be ornaments, furniture, or anything else, should only occur when those items provide you with something. There has to be a practical reason for you to own it, or else you go against the very idea of hygge. If you fail to do this, then you are simply accumulating junk, and junk is pointless.

Those that incorporate hygge into their home believe that everything needs to have a purpose. The table has to be used and not just left in the dining room that simply gathers dust. That TV stand should not block access to your window or other items of furniture. It must have its own position where it can perform its function without any interference.

- **Begin with an Easy Space**

Small wins will help this process be achievable. If it is spring, start with the coat closet and go through all your winter items. Chances are this was something you would have done anyway, so it is a good place to start. If you have children, decide what can be kept for next season and what will be outgrown by then. For adults, take stock of just how many coats you own. It's probably more than you thought.

Often, there is a coat or two that has a broken zipper or a lost button that prevents them from being worn. Be honest with yourself. Are you going to repair these items? If the answer is no, put them in a giveaway box. If the answer is yes, put them in the car so that next time you are running an errand you can drop them off at a tailor.

- **Beware the Junk Drawer**

We all have at least one space in our house, and possibly many, that just accumulates stuff. It's usually in a high-traffic area like the kitchen, and is a place where small items go. The meaning is well. These items are found around the house and are put away because it is better for them to be in a drawer than to be clutter in a different place.

However, what is the purpose of these items? Will we really use them again? Or are they just out of sight and therefore out of mind? Take your time and go through each junk drawer or junk space in your house. Empty everything out and make the following piles:

> – has a home in another place of the house
>
> – garbage
>
> – recycling
>
> – potentially useful for the future
>
> – not useful

Most of the time, these junk items should be relocated. The forgotten crayons belong in your child's room with the other arts supplies. The hair elastic belongs in your bathroom. A lot of junk is papers such as wedding invitations or Christmas cards. While the sentiment of keeping them is nice, if they are just sitting in a drawer without being seen, then they might as well go in the garbage or recycling.

There are some items that should be kept for future use. But be sparing when you keep these. You don't need ten elastic bands. Probably just one or two will do. Be realistic and try to eliminate anything that is not truly useful.

- **Use Technology to Your Advantage**

When it comes to paper, we often think that we need to keep it all, just in case. And some of this is actually true. Receipts are important in case something needs to be returned. Envelopes can have people's addresses that will be needed for future reference. But it's important to understand that the information is needed and not the physical paper.

There are many free apps that will scan and save your receipts for you so that you can throw out the original. Indeed, many stores now offer the option to send the receipt to your email instead of printing you one. Take advantage of this to help declutter your homes.

If there is important information like an address on an envelope, stop and put that in your address book. The same goes with recipes. Instead of having papers ripped from a magazine cluttering everything, sort them into one recipe book. It will make it so much easier for you to find when you want to be creative in the kitchen.

At this point, the objects left are not serving their purpose. Things are in order and have a practical use.

Step 3: Bringing Space and Light into the Home

As we mentioned above, we will look at the concept of de-cluttering in the next chapter, but there's no doubt that when you do remove items from your home, that you then end up with more space. However, it is then a case of what you do with it that's important.

If you look at the typical Scandinavian home, there are some very definite approaches to home décor. There is a sense that the rooms flow together. Light floods in and is bounced around the room by clear and clean surfaces that tend to be light in color. By using light in this way, you open up the room even further and create an illusion of it being more spacious than it really is. Space is important. It helps to create a sense of calm that is often missing in our homes, especially when everything is cramped and we live on top of one another.

The Danes believe in trying to open up natural light as much as possible. Windows are left uncluttered to allow the maximum amount to flood in for as long as nature allows. Furniture is arranged in such a way that anybody can benefit from the light when in the room. It adds character and brings a better atmosphere to the room. It is certainly much better than sitting in darkness.

A hygge home makes use of not only natural light, but also carefully placed artificial lights, and they can come in different forms.

The one thing that the Danes hate is the idea of a large and strong main light that illuminates the entire room. That is harsh, it is overbearing, and it is hardly soothing and relaxing.

Instead, they prefer subtlety with lighting. They prefer light being used in the dark evenings to create a certain mood and feeling about a room. It should add to the atmosphere rather than take anything away from it.

Light should be used to accentuate a room. Candles create a soft glow that will then provide a sense of comfort. Small lights can be carefully positioned in a corner to provide a space to sit and read and relax. Fairy lights dancing across the fireplace to bring it to life even when the fire itself has not been lit. Lights used in furniture with glass fronts to highlight the objects that are on display inside.

You also cannot afford to forget the use of outdoor lighting. Your garden or yard should be a place of pleasure, and lighting can play an important role in that. We are not talking about large spotlights that illuminate every dark corner, but rather lights that enhance your appreciation for your space.

You may wish to include a light on your front porch that makes your door feel more appealing and inviting to guests. In the rear, lights on fence posts casting shadows on aspects of the garden while light dances across the plants is another possibility. You may also wish to incorporate a water feature due to its Zen-like properties, but make sure that it also has a light with it to add to the overall feeling.

In other words, soft and gentle lights outside can add a certain degree of warmth to your entire home. Light makes things seem less threatening, and the outdoors is transformed into a place where you actually want to spend some time and relax.

As you can see, there is a real sense of getting to grips with lighting and using it to your advantage. You need to drop the idea of putting a light in a corner and using it from a purely practical point of view. That just does not work in hygge. There needs to be some thought that goes into the source of light, where it shines, its role, and even how strong it needs to be so it can actually do its job.

Step 4: Dealing with the Space Issue

Even though Danish homes are often relatively small, especially compared to the vast shells that we can often refer to as home, the space that is available in them is mind-blowing.

This is all down to the rather clever way in which rooms are arranged, furniture is designed, and storage is incorporated into each and every room. To those that use hygge in their home, there is nothing that is more claustrophobic than having too many things surrounding you. It creates a sense of the walls closing in and produces a stuffy atmosphere that is hardly relaxing.

Space deals with that problem in an instant. Of course, it does help that materialism is not a big problem in Denmark, so there is not the same plethora of objects to try to cram into our desired space, but at the same time we are also not talking about people with limited belongings that could fit into the proverbial shoebox.

Instead, what we tend to have with people that believe in hygge is the idea of there not being anything in excess. You can own things, but they must serve you. Don't be greedy—do you really need all of those pairs of shoes where several of them are the same style just in different colors?

There is also a need for you to understand the flow of a room and the space that is required that allows you to first of all get to everything, and then for it to be able to be used. This ability to use something becomes more complicated if you have too many belongings that are effectively stacked upon one another.

So, to implement this, you need to be willing to deal with the clutter that you have accumulated over the years. You need to be willing to let things go and to allow them to potentially be moved into a new home where they can perhaps bring joy and pleasure to other people. However, that is for the chapter on de-cluttering, but there is one final aspect of hygge and the home that we need to address.

Step 5: Adding Comfort to Your Home

The fifth and final step that we will discuss at this point is connected to bringing some extra sense of comfort to your home. Now, you might think that you have already achieved this, but as you sit and look around the room that you are currently in, there will more than likely be areas that you are actually not that content with.

This aspect of hygge is so important that we have included it in its very own chapter toward the end of the book. However, at this moment, we can sum up why it plays such a key role in the entire process.

Comfort and coziness trigger a more relaxed response in our mind and body. This allows the muscles to relax and things that may have previously been stressing us out just don't seem to concern us to the same extent.

Chapter 4

Bringing Hygge into the Home

In the previous chapter, we mentioned the idea of de-cluttering your home as being a key part of embracing hygge. However, de-cluttering in hygge can mean so much more than just throwing out the objects in your home.

Instead, we mean looking at your life as a whole and figuring out what is causing you stress, what you do or don't need, the pressures, the expectations, the general things that you do on a day to day basis. If we are all honest, we tend to get involved in things that we would rather avoid or replace with something better. Hygge allows for that, but only when you have de-cluttered your life to begin with.

Let's look at areas that may be of concern to you.

The Home

Okay, so we said at the start of this chapter that there is more to de-cluttering than just dealing with the home, but the home is a good place to start.

Previously, we discussed how we have a tendency to acquire things over time and that there is a reluctance to throw items out. This causes so many problems, and before you know it your home is creaking with all of the objects that you have in your possession.

This is in such opposition to hygge that it is difficult to even know where to begin.

De-cluttering while in a hygge state of mind is about more than simply throwing items out. Even with this action there is a sense of you incorporating the art of mindfulness in what you are doing. You don't just pick up something and throw it in the trash. That is a mindless act, but not in a positive way.

To kickstart this de-cluttering job, you need to have a sense of order in your home. There's no point in moving around without a plan of action. You need to be in the moment and completely aware of the decisions you are making regarding what stays and what is going to be thrown out. Also, consider any item that may be given to someone else or donated to a charity rather than discarding it forever. Just because you are finished with it doesn't necessarily mean that it cannot help another individual.

Step 1: Coming to Terms with Your Belongings

Coming to terms with your belongings is a major first step. Assessing what you own and how much 'stuff' is scattered around is extremely important. Unless you have been actively living a minimalistic way of life for some time, you will be surprised at what you have managed to purchase and own over the years.

As a result, this job could take longer than you were initially expecting.

Be prepared. Make a list of the objects that are in a room. Have no other distractions and focus on the job at hand. Take your time over this, as it is an important part of incorporating hygge into your home life, so you want to get it correct the first time.

Step 2: One Room at a Time

The next step is to only tackle one room at a time. Don't be drawn into thinking about how much work you have to do throughout your home. Instead, focus on the space you are in, and only that space.

That in itself is incorporating both hygge and mindfulness as one, but it also allows you to concentrate on making the correct decisions regarding your belongings.

Step 3: Start Big and Work to Small

In this step, you need to start with the largest objects in the room and decide on the role they play and also whether or not they are practical and even being used correctly. The larger objects that remain will then determine not only the layout of the room, but also what you can then actually keep.

Step 4: Giving Items Away

Consider giving your unnecessary items to someone that would appreciate them, or even to a charity shop that could make some money from their sale. There are many online groups for buying and selling, or even for free items, and it is easier than ever to find a new home for an old item.

No matter if you are giving the item away or if it is broken, you need to think positively of the item as it once served a purpose—even though that purpose is now different. There is a sense of giving it thanks for its service to you and acknowledge in your mind that it is now time to bring new things into that space that will serve a brand-new purpose. Also, the art of exchanging items with others is something that should not be forgotten. It is regarded as being very friendly, and as we will see throughout this book, being friendly is a huge part of hygge.

Once again, you must think about the space an item takes up as well as the position in the room. Does it get in the way and are you constantly bumping into it? Is it broken in any way? If so, first look to fix it and give it a new life. If it can't be fixed, then let it go

Work out these large things first, and the rest will then become so much easier.

Dealing with Friends and Social Situations

Perhaps you have a social life that is frenetic and doesn't provide you with time for yourself. For this, you must ask yourself why you are being drawn into doing so many things. Are you unable to say no or are you worried about doing so?

Too often, we can be pulled into situations or positions that we would have rather avoided. It puts added stress on our body and mind, and yet we push ourselves even though it is extremely uncomfortable inside.

Those who believe in the concept of hygge won't do this. It helps when everybody is on the same page regarding this as people are not as concerned about coming across as being cold or unfriendly if they are unwilling to participate in something. Instead, the Danes will just accept that there are other things that people wish to do or deal with and they don't take it personally. There is an acceptance that you have to put your own self first on most occasions, and this is not even regarded as being selfish as it is still done with a kind heart.

However, we will discuss friends and their role a bit more in the next chapter.

There is also the idea in hygge that you need to de-clutter your mind of those thoughts that are intrusive, and yet also pointless. We tend to bring additional stress into our life that is just not required, so it is clear that there is a need to look at those stresses and determine how they can be removed. That alone is a good enough explanation as to why hygge and mindfulness work so well together. It is almost as if they are twins in some sense. One works in perfect harmony with the other, but only when clutter is not all-consuming.

Chapter 5

Friends and Their Role in Your Life

Friends play an integral role in hygge. However, that's only the case when they actually provide you with something.

This isn't to say that you should only spend time with someone if they can give you 'things.' Instead, it's more about something that is nurturing in some respect. You need to seek friendships that have a give and take concept rather than friends who just take, take, and take some more. Those friends do not lend themselves to the concept of hygge. They add stress and ill-feeling—two things that you always want to avoid.

So, how do you determine the friends to keep and the role that they are then going to play in your life?

Social Media Friend Types

Let's start with something that is still relatively new in the history of humankind—social media. Look at your list of friends on Facebook. They all serve a purpose, but whether that purpose is positive or negative, remains to be seen. Here are some typical types of friends you may have via social media and how to best use this means of communication.

- **Family**
- share pictures (either publicly or privately) of children for grandparents to see their daily progress
- create group chats so siblings can stay connected and talk freely
- share new stories that might interest others

- **Good Friends**
- -create events to help determine what dates work best
- -share recipes and helpful advice
- -enjoy seeing their family moments

- **Old Friends**
- -share stories or pictures and reminisce about childhood and school
- -plan meet-ups once a year to stay in touch and relive good times
- -keep up to date with what they are doing so that even if a while passes before you can see them again, you still feel like a part of their lives

- **Online Only Friends**
- -accept that you don't have time to socialize in person, but acknowledge that you still respect them
- -remember how and where you met them and their importance in that time of your life

- **Negative People that Upset You**
- -realize that there will always be people that have different views than you
- -accept that you can't change other people; you can only change yourself
- -move on from them and remove them from your life, both online and in person

Different people serve different purposes. It is ok to have a lot of people you are friends with on social media. Just make sure those people are more than just a number. Use the essence of hygge to acknowledge how they make your life better. If they don't, then there is no point to keeping them around.

The Role Friends Should Play

Friends should be people that you enjoy being around. Nothing should feel forced. In Denmark, people make a point of spending time with their closest friends on a regular basis. They swap stories, share their thoughts on various subjects, and the entire event is a relaxed, enjoyable time where you feel as if you have connected with people.

Everybody has an ease with how they get on with one another. There is no sense of someone being better than somebody else. Flaunting your wealth or being materialistic is frowned upon.

Friends should bring a sense of warmth to the table. In hygge, every individual should have different people that they know they can turn to when they have problems that they wish to share. They know the individual in their social circle that can help them from a relationship point of view, or a problem at work, or whatever may be wrong.

This sense of being relaxed around people due to the way in which you trust them with so many of your secrets helps to calm the mind and make life seem so much easier to bear. It does take on the concept that 'a problem shared is a problem halved' and we are all aware of how that alone can relax the mind and make things seem as if they are not so bad after all.

How Friends Work in Hygge

This heading may sound peculiar, but there is an actual art to the way in which the Danes approach friendships and incorporate them into hygge. Now, you would be forgiven for thinking that this was all about being cozy and comfortable, and it does still apply in this instance.

We mentioned how friends need to provide you with something, and if you think about the earlier chapters regarding objects and items, you can see how dealing with your friends can fall under the same rules and regulations.

To provide you with a better explanation, we can head back to Denmark and look at what happens with friendships and the way in which people come together. Clearly, they are experts at incorporating the concepts of hygge into their interactions, so we should seek to learn a substantial amount from them.

For the Danes, meeting up with friends is not only done on a regular occasion, but it is also a joyous event every single time. The atmosphere is one that is laid back and relaxed with nobody cast as the outsider; everyone is involved and made to feel welcome. Indeed, this sense of making people feel welcome extends to those that you live near to as well, so there is a real community feel to the place, and this is something that you should seek to incorporate into your very own attempts at hygge.

To further stress how friends work, we can paint a picture of a typical gathering in Denmark. Remember, this can happen every single week, so while we have a tendency to try to gather as many friends as possible, the Danes prefer a more minimalistic approach. It is more about the quality of the friends rather than how many of them that you appear to have that is important.

So, once a week, friends will either get together to go off and enjoy an experience, or they will look at meeting up at the home of one of the group with this often happening on a rotating basis. Once together, there will be several drinks, some food to eat, and a tendency to discuss things and life in general. Some people also prefer to add in some music to help with the atmosphere, so that is certainly worth considering.

For the décor, it does depend on the time of day, but on a number of occasions it will be the afternoon for obvious work-related reasons. However, you should still look at making things as comfortable as possible, no matter how many people may be about to visit you.

With the soft furnishings aspect, you may want to consider more cushions that are plumper and have real feathers inside. They feel much better, as well as look more impressive. Lighting is clearly going to play a role, and the Danes will go back to what they know best, which includes fairy lights and a plethora of candles. It adds to the atmosphere and makes everything seem more relaxed.

Remember, if you are nice and relaxed, then it is harder for people to try to pull the wool over your eyes as the mind is so much sharper. That is the one thing that everybody tries to attain when they have friends over, so do think about the personalities of the individuals that will be there and make sure that the atmosphere you are trying to achieve fits in well with the majority of the group.

It may sound as if there is a lot of internal politics when it comes to this, but that is actually not the case. Hygge focuses on being careful with each and every aspect of friends coming together.

Steps to Implement

At the end of most chapters, we are looking at several steps that you might want to take should you wish to go ahead and implement some of the points that were made during the chapter.

In this instance, the main steps are related to not having too many friends and clearing out those on social media that just sit there and bring nothing to your own particular table. Social media should be an extension of your real life. Instead of trying to collect the most amount of friends, look for meaningful relationships.

Also, with the friends that nurture you and provide you with the kind of friendship you are looking for, you must make sure that you do not allow that friendship to slip on by. It's a case of keeping in touch with people, showing an interest, and not doing it from a distance, if at all possible.

Facebook is good at reminding you when a friend's birthday is, but instead of simply typing in a quick 'happy birthday,' think about how you can bring a real smile to that friend's day. Post a meaningful picture of the two of you that brings up fond memories. Or better yet, call and have a conversation with your friend. Showing an interest isn't about grand gestures. Rather, it is about caring enough to make an extra effort.

The Danes believe that these close friendships nurture the soul and improve life. These friendships should be allowed to grow and develop. Meeting up with friends should be something to look forward to and treasure. It should be done on a regular basis due entirely to the various positives associated with the experience. It should be a perfect blend between the idea of hygge and friendship.

Chapter 6

The Idea of Experiences

Life is an experience. This is very much an accepted concept in Denmark where they attempt to make the most of things even in those cold and dark winter months where many others would effectively hibernate until winter has passed.

For the Danes, this is not an option. It is simply a case of being better prepared and dealing with it, for that is part of the experience that they wish to have.

When we talk about experiences, we mean something that happens to us. This is in contrast to something that just happens. Watching TV is not an experience. The TV is on, we watch it, and hopefully we gain enjoyment from it, but nothing really happens.

Instead, think of experiences where you are active. This can be either physically, mentally, or both. Experiences can be with other people or on our own. They should be enjoyable, but that does not mean they have to be easy.

If you're not sure where to begin with an experience, narrow your daily life into during the week and the weekends.

After work, what happens? You come home, make dinner, and then have a few hours before going to sleep. Is this time full of experiences or just a place holder until bedtime? Experiences don't have to be big or all-consuming. They can be as simple as an evening stroll or reading a book.

Often, this evening time is spent watching TV. There's nothing wrong with TV, but it's a good idea to minimize the amount you watch. If you find that the TV automatically goes on after dinner, try moving the TV to a different room. If you have to physically go into another room to watch it, then it becomes more of a conscious choice that is made.

As for the weekends, start by organizing your time into three compartments: errands and important tasks, social time, and relaxing time. Try to incorporate all three into each weekend to provide balance in your life. Some weekends may be heavier in a specific category, and that's ok.

Vacations are exciting experiences and they are often viewed as a once a year event. And while this can be a great opportunity to see the world, you can also schedule smaller vacations throughout the year. Try to take a half day on Friday and explore a neighboring city for the weekend. It is amazing what you can discover that is close to home.

It will perhaps be no surprise to discover that the experience itself should be fulfilling in some way. It should nurture the soul or the mind. It should bring a sense of happiness to you that had previously been lacking. It should provide you with fond memories that you can then recall and recant the tale to others some years further down the line.

It is about enjoying life no matter what your limitations may be. Find joy in the simplest of things rather than placing too much expectation on an event or location. Doing so will only increase the potential chances of you failing to enjoy the experience, and yet it can be so easy to avoid this happening.

When trying to abide by the relatively lax laws of hygge, it can sometimes be difficult to work out how to include hygge into the idea of experiences. In this chapter, we will explain it more fully, and perhaps even give you some ideas of how you can then proceed in your own life.

Getting to Grips with the Correct Experiences

If we plan on sticking closely to the concept of hygge, then we have to approach this idea of experiences from a certain direction. In short, an experience must provide us with something positive or nurturing. It cannot afford to put pressure on us, make us anxious in a negative way, or send our stress levels soaring.

An experience doing these things would be directly working against hygge as a concept.

Clearly, the next step has to, therefore, involve you being aware of how to identify the correct experiences for your own self. There is only person that will be able to do that, and it is you. Nobody else can help, although some guidance can be offered.

Finding Something that Satisfies Your Soul

With experiences and hygge, there has to be some connection between what it is that you are doing or experiencing and how it benefits your soul. That is why there is a real need for you to understand what you enjoy and what would be a positive experience for you.

There is no point in us sitting there producing a list. After all, we are all different in what we like and enjoy. What pleases your soul will not necessarily work, even for somebody else in your family.

One of the best ways to approach this concept of finding something for the sake of your soul is to look at getting a quiet spot in your home and clearing your mind of all of the external thoughts that are putting pressure on you. This is a time for reflection and working out what your goals are, or the things that would, in effect, appear on your bucket list. Ask yourself a whole host of questions connected to what you like, desire, or any other emotion that is positive in nature. You then need to determine the kind of experience that goes with those emotions.

Organization is Key

You may have already come to the conclusion that a lot of hygge involves being organized. This approach also applies when you are looking at experiences. Yes, it may be argued by some that off the cuff experiences are wonderful things to have, but you cannot always rely on them.

If we take ourselves back to Denmark and look at the way in which the Danes often approach activities, then what we see is that there is a tendency to think things through so that the experience goes as smoothly as possible. There is no point in having an experience if all it does is increase your stress levels.

Plan ahead, as much as possible, and look at all of the ways in which things could potentially go wrong. You want to counteract this as best you can, and as quickly as possible, so that things go smoothly. Remember, if things work well, then you will enjoy the experience even more, and this applies no matter the size or the scale of the experience that you are talking about.

Size Doesn't Matter

Before we finish this chapter, we want to get one thing straight. When we are talking about the concept of experiences, we are not always talking about a massive event that is going to completely change your life.

An experience does not need to be of any large size. For the Danes, something as simple as having a nice cup of coffee in a cozy coffee shop that is warm, snug, and comfortable is an experience to behold. If you then add into the equation a nice view and friendly atmosphere, then you have something that warms both the heart and the soul.

Alternatively, you might just enjoy taking your dog for a walk in the cold fresh air and spending the time absorbing the nature that is all around you. This will allow your mind to drift into the areas that it wants you to be. Small experiences can be just as important as big ones.

We are not talking about skydiving or swimming with sharks, although there is nothing to stop you from doing either of those things if that is what you would prefer. However, experiences that incorporate hygge into them tend to be more nurturing and wholesome. It is no surprise that we included a chapter on friends, thanks to the role that they play in the entire concept of experiences.

However, never feel obliged to include friends or family in your experiences. Experiences really should be very personal to you, and you alone. If you wish to include them, then that's your decision. At the same time, the rules of hygge would argue that it is then up to the individuals to respect your decision for what it is, and not through any particular affiliation.

Also, there is a feeling amongst those practitioners of hygge, that an experience does not have to be linked to one single part. Instead, they prefer to go ahead and look at each and every aspect. This may include getting to the experience, who is there, what happens after the experience, and so much more. Overall, there is the belief that you need to allow yourself to be absorbed into the moment, which takes us back to the whole idea of mindfulness and the way in which it is clearly linked to hygge.

The Steps to Take in This Instance

Having the correct experiences, and doing so within the confines of hygge, will be straightforward enough for most people. However, there are certain steps that should, by all accounts, be followed.

First, accept that you don't have to satisfy all of your interests or wishes for experiences at one time. This is all about enjoying it, and making the most of it and then moving on to the next experience.

Next, understand that the experience must be born from your own wishes. Having an experience just to satisfy others does not necessarily work.

Always plan and organize things to the best of your ability. This should make sure that the experience is better than it otherwise would be, and remember that this is also the approach that hygge encourages you to take with anything and everything that you do.

Chapter 7

Hygge can Extend to the Workplace

Now, this may sound as if it will be a strange chapter regarding hygge, but it is entirely possible for you to incorporate the hygge approach even in your place of work.

If you stop to think about this for a second, you'll realize that bringing hygge to the workplace is actually a good thing to do. After all, the workplace is often regarded as being one of the more stressful areas of our lives, and yet we cannot avoid it.

Well, the truth is that you can avoid it, but not by quitting your job. Instead, by applying some of the concepts of hygge to your workplace, it is entirely possible for you to transform the energy that surrounds you. As a result, it will become a far more pleasant place, and one that you will perhaps enjoy from time to time, although nothing can be guaranteed.

Clearly, there is some work to be done in order to transform your workplace, and there are a number of important steps that one must follow to ultimately end up with a more relaxed atmosphere.

Step 1: Coming to Grips with the Issues

Before you can fix anything or bring hygge into the workplace, you need to be aware of what the issues are, so they can then be addressed. Issues could be about the space where you work. Issues may lie with some of your colleagues. Issues could be about the way in which you approach your job and are filled with uncertainties and insecurities that spill over into stress and a hatred for what you do.

For this step, sit back and take a moment to think things over about your place of work. What kind of things stress you out? Where are the problems that you would love to resolve?

Clearly, it is impossible for us to cover each and every issue that people may have at their place of work. However, taking the time to study your working environment, the people you interact with, and even the pressures you are under will help to point you in the right direction for whatever it is that needs to be addressed.

Remember, hygge is often about looking at yourself and determining what brings you comfort and happiness. You may be able to learn about some things that can influence you, but aside from that, your success with hygge really does rest on your own shoulders.

That being said, we can look at some areas to help you to come to terms with the way in which hygge can be incorporated into your working life.

Looking at the Workplace

Next, we will look at the workplace and how you can make things better and more comfortable. Now, this is clearly going to depend on the type of work that you do, so it's not always going to be possible to incorporate all of these suggested aspects of hygge, but we can try to give you some tips that may be useful.

For this, we can look at several scenarios. The idea is that you will then have some examples to work from and to implement in your own place of work—as long as they correspond with what makes you feel more relaxed and comfortable, of course.

If you have a desk job, then including the concept of hygge into your workplace is very easy. In the next chapter, we will look at adding some comfort into your life, since this is a huge part of hygge, but we can offer a summary at this point.

Your desk should be organized and everything ought to be in order. It should not be cluttered or contain items that are useless. You should be able to find anything you want at any point. Your chair should be comfortable and supportive. There should be adequate lighting. Your desk should be at the correct height for your needs. Also, any equipment should be in working order.

If your workplace is primarily in a vehicle, then there are still things you can do that will make your office on wheels far more comfortable.

First, there should still be a sense of organization involved. Your case or bag should contain everything you need and you should be able to access it easily. You should keep your car clean and neat as well as looking at ways to make your journey as comfortable as possible. The road is stressful, so hygge enthusiasts would look for ways to make driving more calming and relaxing, perhaps by having comforting music.

As you can see, there are several common threads between these two examples. You must focus on comfort, being organized, and keeping things clean and neat.

Dealing with Work Colleagues

Even though your work colleagues may not be regarded as friends, there are still some rules that are connected to hygge that will help you to potentially get through a difficult part of your working life.

It is impossible, unless you work in a very small location, for every individual to always get on well with one another all of the time. That is just asking too much.

However, when using hygge, you need to look at things from a different perspective with your work colleagues.

First, be aware of what they bring to your place of work. Ask yourself what their role is and how it impacts your own role. Spend time thinking about what they bring you, and also the level of interaction that you actually need to have with them. This is especially important when you perhaps do not see eye to eye some of the time, but as you cannot exactly ignore them, it does make a difference if you understand how to approach this situation.

The Danes will deal with this type of problem in a typically calm way. First, there is an acceptance that some people just do not click with one another, but there should be a form of mutual respect in the workplace for what each person brings to the company or organization. If you can accept this, even without fully accepting the person, then you are part of the way toward resolving the issue.

Next, the Danes would work at allowing old issues to stay in the past. Remember that hygge involves mindfulness, which is all about staying in the moment, and this also applies to the ways in which you interact with people.

If an individual at work is upsetting you, but you still have to deal with them, then the Danish idea would be to work with them, finish the job or interaction, and then move on and turn your attention elsewhere. Lingering on bad thoughts serves no purpose and it stresses the mind, which is completely unnecessary.

In other words, hygge can teach you how to work alongside people that you are not particularly fond of, just by getting you to focus your mind in a specific way. Acceptance and forgiveness are key points, and if you can work with those in mind, then even those individuals that are particularly irritating will become less significant as a result.

Hygge and Your Career

Finally, we should briefly look at the role that hygge can, and should, play in your career.

Too often, people get caught up in the daily grind of the nine to five job, and they hate it. They see work as a chore and start watching the clock from the moment they arrive. Lunch hour is the best hour of the day, and all that they can think of is their salary at the end of the month. It is depressing—and that is not even including the journey to and from work alongside what feels like the rest of the population of the planet at the same time.

As you would expect, this cannot be described as hygge.

So, how can the two possibly work together? Well, the answer is about using what makes you feel happy, content, and includes things that you enjoy doing. It tells you to find your strengths and passions and work on them so that they become a central part of your entire approach to your working life.

Look at what you do for a living. You may very well be lucky and be in the profession that you trained for, but you need to work out if you are content with your actual position.

For example, perhaps you are a teacher. You may have wanted to teach your entire life as you love being in education and you have a passion for it. Even with this, you might want to ask yourself if you enjoy the school you work at or the salary you receive. Also, there may be an issue with the level of teaching you are working at because perhaps you want to be higher up, maybe in administration or in teacher training.

Or, there may be times where you wish to be your own boss and run your own company. You may be stressed about the way that your boss treats you, and you feel as if there is no respect. In this instance, hygge followers would believe that you should go down the path of the type of work that makes your life feel better and less stressful.

In short, staying in a job that brings you unhappiness and stress is not an option. It is said that switching to a more calming situation, or with better people, will make going to work less of a chore, and this alone is worth taking a reduction in salary.

Look at it this way—the Danes are not known for working long hours. They also refuse to generally do any overtime, and they do not feel bad about it. Now, compare that to other countries and societies where overtime is almost expected. Also, what happens if you say no? There is often the fear of being fired, or overlooked for promotions or bonuses. It is no surprise that the Danes, aside from being the happiest nation in the world, are also amongst the happiest workers in the world.

They have the correct balance between working life and personal life. They work fewer hours, but are then far more productive during their working schedule. This work rate is all connected to the simple fact that they feel content with their careers, and the production levels are the direct result of that happiness.

Now, if only we could incorporate those ideas into more businesses and companies, then there would be a real positive shift in the economy.

Chapter 8

Adding Some Comfort into Your Life

At this point, we are going to spend some time talking not about a specific aspect of your life, but a more general theme. That theme is comfort, because including it in your daily life is going to heal your mind and soul, which are both so very important when dealing with hygge.

Immediately, your mind will conjure up various images of what is comfortable to you, and that is good as it gives you something to work on. However, you need to also take into account how easy it is to incorporate those ideas into your life. Do remember that one of the main principles of hygge is the way in which anybody should be able to do it and feel a positive change in their life. They should really be capable of feeling that this sense of comfort is something that you can learn once you explore your own senses and sensual side.

Of course, you will perhaps still be sitting there wondering how you can bring comfort in your life, and you may even have no idea about where to begin. If so, then let's break it down into nice and easy points.

Coming to Terms with Stressors

This is a point that has been brought up in several of the chapters above, but it makes so much sense for you to understand your stressors in order to then counteract them and include more comfort in your life. This applies no matter how big or small the stressor may be, although you need to be aware of how you should never expect to completely eliminate all stress, because that is impossible.

As hygge is primarily focused on de-stressing your life, it helps you to know the areas in which you have to work on, compared to those that are perhaps best left alone. After all, the benefits that you will receive as a result of overcoming those stressors is going to be huge.

But here is something important: throughout this book, we have largely focused on different aspects of life from the home, to friends, and even the workplace. Not one single area is more important than the other. They all blend together seamlessly to provide a more satisfactory life. However, accepting that we do indeed have stressors allows us to then move on and make progress.

But, of course, one has to understand the areas and what to do in order to solve those issues, which is what we will look at now.

Starting with Your Own Self

Trying to make things more comfortable around you is pointless if you are not that comfortable with yourself. A lack of understanding what makes you happy and content will only prove to make this entire idea of hygge so much harder than before.

There must be a sense of contentment within you. There must be a sense of you being aware of what makes you happy or sad, and then incorporating the correct things into your life.

By all accounts, you should be happy with your home, friendships, relationships, and working life even though, at times, such happiness might seem like an impossible dream. Of course, there will be times where it is difficult and troublesome, but then the Danes will view these problems from a less stressed point of view, which is clearly more beneficial for you to then deal with the problem at hand.

Think about what brings you joy and pleasure, and then actively go after those things as the boost that they will give you will be substantial. If you are comfortable within your own skin, then anything external suddenly becomes so much easier to cope with, and you will be less stressed in the process.

This will involve you looking closely at yourself and having the ability to accept that changes may have to be made. You need to be relatively self-critical as that is the only way to then force you into seeking the changes that need to be made to improve your situation.

Remember, hygge is all about getting that sense of comfort within yourself. It is about that sense of self satisfaction that is often missing in our lives. One has to take the time to figure out what provides us with that satisfaction, and to then seek out ways in which we are able to attain that. Yes, it sounds impossible at times, but then hygge is also about taking your time and making sure that you do things right.

If it takes you days or weeks of sitting and thinking about what satisfies you, or what changes you need to make, then that is absolutely fine. After all, putting additional pressure and stress on your own shoulders will directly contradict the whole idea of hygge.

Comfort and the Home

When adding that sense of comfort to your home, there is a very real need for you to have carried out the first step, which is dealing with yourself, before you turn your attention in this direction.

It is all too easy for one to feel swamped and overwhelmed with what they feel they need to do when it comes to the home and producing that cozy and comfortable feeling. However, the process is straightforward; just as long as you have set aside the time in order to deal with each and every room.

It would take too long for us to go through each and every room offering examples of how to add a sense of comfort to them, but a number of general concepts will be enough to give you an idea of how to proceed.

Idea 1: Space and Flow

We mentioned the idea of space and flow in the chapter on the home, but there's no doubt that it does bring a sense of comfort and ease to the room, which is why we are mentioning it once again. Simply the fact that you can use everything that you have and there is no difficulty in doing so adds its own sense of comfort. Cast your mind back to how annoying it can be when you have to move items to get to what you want.

It then becomes easier to see how removing a particular obstacle will make things far more comfortable.

Idea 2: Start at the Entrance

In hygge, you want to feel at home and relaxed from the moment you walk in your front door. Some take it further and include even just walking up to the front door, but that is something that is up to you.

However, think of this example: you have had a bad day and are stressed. You are back home and walking to your front door. All you want to do is get in, throw off your shoes, and close the world off from you to allow yourself a break. However, several obstacles are in the way, such as a messy entryway, no clear space to set down keys or handbag, or dull lighting that might cause you to trip on the step.

This all sounds commonplace, and unfortunately it is, but not for those individuals who have included hygge into their life. Instead, they have made their home feel far more comfortable as soon as they open that door. A warm rug, soft lighting, a place to put your shoes and to hang up your coat. If it gets cold, then a heater of some kind would be easily switched on so you are welcomed by warmth.

In addition, there may be a special scent that relaxes you so you smell it as soon as you arrive. Comfortable footwear or warm socks are ready to be put on.

All of this adds to you feeling far more comfortable than you were up until that point. It sets a good standard for the rest of your home, although you still need to follow through with incorporating hygge into each area.

Idea 3: Bringing Soft Lights into the Equation

We mentioned light earlier, but it bears repeating because of the great impact that soft lighting can have on the atmosphere and feeling in the home.

Danes buy the most candles of anyone in the world, and this is directly attributed to hygge. They understand how that small, flickering light can add so much feeling to an entire room by having it lighting up a small corner at a time.

At the same time, there is something magical about dimmer lights rather than going for the full spotlight effect that some individuals have in their home.

Idea 4: Adding that Extra Sense of Warmth

This can be done no matter where you live, so if you think warmth it is only for those individuals who experience cold, dark winters, then think again.

Bringing warmth to your home can take on many different forms. For warmth, we are not only talking about throws and blankets or those comfortable socks to keep your toes from freezing up. Instead, it can also be about the colors on the walls. The rugs on the wooden floors. The fireplace that may, or may not, purely be for show, but which can still add a certain atmosphere to a room.

It is about a fluffy duvet and huge pillows on your bed. It is about those thick towels that you wrap yourself in after a shower. A snug and soft dressing gown. There are so many ideas that give that sense of warmth, and hygge wants you to embrace as many of them as possible.

Comfort and Your Friends

We have also mentioned friends and how they fit into the concept of hygge, but you will be wondering how we can tie in this comfort point of view as well. Clearly, it takes some abstract thinking to work through it, but it's easier than you think.

When we talk about comfort and friends, what we mean is that you feel at ease in their company. You feel that you can be yourself and don't need to put up some facade to placate them and their own problems. Of course, you need to be sympathetic with people and display empathy, but there still has to be a real sense of you being at ease when with them.

That is why hygge will teach you to think carefully about the friends that you have. Be aware of your shared interests or common goals. Why are you friends with them in the first place?

Be aware of how your personalities either get on or clash, because if they do clash or there is some strain in the relationship, then it's best to think about moving away from them as friends.

Instead, to keep in line with this comfort principle, our advice is to focus on the reason for the friendship and determine how you feel around them. If there is any tension, either by what they do or how they act that makes you uncomfortable, then that is not exactly hygge.

You are best to include individuals that bring warmth and a relaxed atmosphere to your life. Those are the people who fit in best with hygge and the individual friendships that you should try to continue to nurture as much as possible.

Comfort and Experiences

Moving on to the experiences section, we see that there are similarities with what we have said regarding friends and friendships. The main aim is to look at those experiences that will nurture you and can be cherished in the future. A sense of joy and happiness that stays with you for some length of time is the part that you must aim for.

With hygge, there is also a sense of you pushing your own comfort levels, as that is the only way in which you can entice yourself into trying out new things. Yes, there is something to be said about staying within your boundaries as they are seen as being safe, but there is more to life than that, and hygge tells you to experience life rather than missing out on it.

For the sake of experiences, it is best if you understand your own limitations and don't necessarily go past them. Search for enjoyment within those boundaries, but test them on a regular basis. The sense of achievement and pleasure that you get from this cannot be underestimated. It fits in perfectly with the hygge concept of enjoying life and getting the most out of it that you can, without stressing yourself out, of course.

Comfort and the Workplace

This may very well be the hardest one, but it is possible to provide yourself with a greater sense of comfort within your place of work. Clearly, if you are unhappy at what you do, then followers of hygge would argue that you should change your career. Changing jobs might be the only way to get away from some potentially bad and stressful situations, so it should never be ruled out as a possibility.

However, aside from changing where you work, there are other things you can do that will indeed bring a sense of comfort into your place of work.

First, if you work at a desk, you need to think about having things arranged perfectly. That means you don't have to search for items and stress yourself out, and also think about how you are sitting and whether or not that can be improved. For example, some Danes will add cushions or seek a chair that is ergonomically designed for added comfort. This type of design means that it fits their back perfectly, so there is no slouching or anything else that can place added strain on their posture.

Also, you may want to look at the height of your workstation and determine how it fits in with your perfect working height. Remember, if you are sitting there for a considerable length of time, then you want to make sure that even your desk is working well for you.

Think about bringing in something fun and relaxing. Perhaps a plant, a photo or reminder of the family, or anything else that will bring a sense of comfort to your workspace.

As you can see, there are a whole host of ways in which you can bring a sense of comfort into your life no matter the area that you are talking about. It is simply a case of spending the time figuring out what gives you comfort, and then putting a plan into action.

Remember, comfort is a very personal thing. Be aware of your own preferences and work toward them on a regular basis. Incorporating hygge into your life is a continual thing, so make the most of it whenever possible.

Chapter 9

Bringing it All Together

Throughout this book on hygge, we have sought to introduce you to this particular way of life. We have shown that there are more aspects to it than just making sure your home is a peaceful place to live. Instead, your friends, the experiences you have, and where you work can all be influenced by this way of thinking.

You have to admit that there has to be something special about the entire concept if the Danes are continually the happiest people in the world. They themselves even attribute their happiness to hygge, so surely we should listen to the people at the top of the happiness tree while the rest of us are contemplating how to move higher up the branches.

So, what do you do?

The best approach is undoubtedly to try to bring the various aspects of hygge together into one solid, peaceful union. Each part of your life should work in tandem, and you need to be in the moment so that you are indeed fulfilled.

We started off by looking at mindfulness, and a recurring theme throughout these chapters has been looking closely at yourself in order to find the answers that you seek. There is a need to have a strong understanding of what you want or like in life, and then know how to get it. However, never believe for one moment that this is materialistic, as that is not the case. Instead, hygge is the antithesis of materialism, so if you desire to own a collection of thirty Chanel bags, then hygge may not be for you.

De-cluttering and stripping things back to basic levels can free both your mind and soul. It's no surprise that some people view hygge as a cleansing ritual as mind and body can both be affected by clutter in different ways.

The entire idea here is to create the calm and peaceful life that appears to be at odds with how modern life is portrayed. The rush for more wealth and things in order to satisfy something inside of us, or at times to be used as bragging rights for others, is not at all in line with hygge. The Danes are not known for acting like this, and it is probably then not a surprise that they are so happy.

Look at your home, your life, your own soul, friends, relationships, experiences, and your working life to ultimately get a clear picture of who you are as a person. That is the groundwork that is required for an attempt to incorporate hygge into your life to be successful. Make a plan. Know the areas where you are lacking and seek out ways to counteract this and potentially make them your strong point.

Hygge can be fun, but you need to have a firm understanding of what you are doing. So, to round things off in this chapter, we will look at the key points that stand out for us over and above every other aspect of hygge as a whole.

- Focus on the art of mindfulness.
- You need to be in the moment and understand what something or someone does for you.
- Start by looking at your own self before moving outwards.
- Turn your home into the relaxing space that you have always wanted.
- Bring comfort and coziness to your home.
- Begin at the front door so you get that comfortable feeling as soon as you enter.
- Don't forget the outside, either, so your home looks pleasant and welcoming.
- De-clutter, and do it immediately.
- Fix broken things.
- Remember that everything must serve a purpose.
- Each object must also have its own place without getting in the way.
- You must allow both space and light to enter each and every room.
- Use soft light rather than full light, as it provides a better atmosphere.
- Your friends are not going to be immune from being cleared out.
- Look at experiences that nurture you.

- Don't forget your workplace, and make it as comfortable as you can.

There are many other things that we have covered in this e-book, but the points above give you an indication of what to expect when you set out to apply the concepts of hygge in your daily life. Of course, it is up to you to make of it what you will.

Conclusion

There you have it, the basics of hygge in different areas of your life. As you can imagine, this endeavor is something that requires some thought on your part, so don't fall into the belief that you will be able to change things in an instant.

When you stop and think about it, the fact that we understand what it is that makes the Danes so happy is quite cool. It is especially cool when you factor in that anybody can implement various aspects of hygge into their lives and get the benefit of it in an instant. Yes, it is hard work and you will make some mistakes, or let things slide along the way, but that is only to be expected. Indeed, the Danes would shrug their shoulders and allow that moment to pass them by as they understand that more important things are just around the corner.

You don't need to spend money to incorporate hygge. You don't need to be some huge interior designer to make your home feel spacious or to include better lighting. You don't need to be a party animal with a social media account that is straining at the seams.

All you need is to understand what makes you happy and to then have the conviction to have those elements in your life on a regular basis. There is no secret formula to apply–the secret is inside of you. As a result, you are the only person who is aware of this, or even knows what you are truly like.

Hygge has the ability to make your life happier. It will de-stress and de-clutter your life in more ways than you could ever imagine. It will help you to appreciate what you have in life, and also assist you in letting go of what you don't want. You will know the friendships to develop and the individuals to cherish.

However, more importantly, you will be aware of your life becoming easier as you move further into the idea. Comfort is everything in hygge, so accept it and enjoy it as this is a feeling that you could probably get quite used to.

To conclude, hygge is good for your soul. It is also exceptionally good for your mind, so choose methods that best fit in with your own particular needs or wants. Avoid listening to what others tell you. This is on your shoulders, so if there are any issues, then you know who to talk to about it.

Hygge has made the Danes the happiest people alive in the world. That in itself is a major accolade and with the various potential options that are open to you, it's no wonder that you might now feel excited about what the new day may bring.

The only final word of warning is that you need to pay close attention to each and every part of incorporating hygge into your life. Assess how you feel, and then act accordingly. If it is good enough for the Danes, then it is going to be good enough for you. Embrace hygge, and embrace happiness.

One last thing before you go – Can I ask a small favor? I need your help! If this book has been helpful to you, could you share your experience on Amazon by providing an honest feedback and review? This wouldn't take much of your time (a sentence will be very much appreciated), but a massive help for me and absolutely good Karma. Due to not having the backing of a big publication I don't have the big reach or promotion to get my books out to a bigger audience and rely heavily on my readers help, I take out time to read every review and I'm usually extremely excited for every honest feedback I get. If my book was able to inspire you, please express it! This will help position me at the top for others seeking for new ideas and reasonable knowledge to access easily.

I'm very grateful and I wish you every good things of life on your journey!

Warm regards,

Thomas.

My Free Gift to You – <u>Get One of My Audiobooks For Free!</u>

If you've never created an account on Audible (the biggest audiobook store in the world), **<u>you can claim one free</u>** audiobook **<u>of mine!</u>**

It's a simple process:

1. Pick one of audiobooks on Audible:

https://www.audible.com/search?keywords=thomas+nielson&ref=a_search_t1_header_search

or search for Thomas Nielson in Audible

2. Once you choose a book and open its detail page click the orange button "Free with 30-Day Trial Membership."

3. Follow the instructions to create you account and download you first free audiobook.

Not that you are NOT obligated to continue after your free trial expires. You can cancel you free trial easily anytime and won't be charged at all.

About The Author

Hi there, Thomas here.

My life has been one fulfilling and amazing journey, one which I want to share and have everyone to be a part of or at least experience in one way or the other. I'm a firm believer that we still have a lot to give and learn despite our premade beliefs. I want to share all my experiences and hoping it helps you in one way or another.

Living and growing up in Denmark has given me so many good things and experiences that I never thought would be something of value to someone else until I started travelling and meeting new people. While talking to new friends I told them about my home country, the way I lived and the mindset I had, they were amazed and wanted to know more.

I decided that the best way to help them was not only ell them but write it all down for them and since that day I have shared things I feel which will be valuable.

Life doesn't have to be stressful, keep calm and live life.